THE CLASSICAL COOKBOOK

THE CLASSICAL COOKBOOK

Andrew Dalby and Sally Grainger

THE BRITISH MUSEUM PRESS

© 1996, 2012 Andrew Dalby and Sally Grainger

First published 1996
Second (revised) edition published in 2012 by
The British Museum Press
A division of The British Museum Company Ltd
38 Russell Square
London WC1B 3QQ

britishmuseum.org/publishing

Andrew Dalby and Sally Grainger have asserted their rights to be identified
as the authors of this work

ISBN: 978 0 7141 2275 5

A catalogue record for this book is available from the British Library

Designed by Simon Daley at Giraffe Books

Printed in China by C&C Offset Printing Co., Ltd

The papers used by the British Museum Press are recyclable products and the
manufacturing processes are expected to conform to the environmental regulations
of the country of origin.

The vast majority of the objects illustrated in this book are from the collection of the
British Museum. The registration number for each of these items is given at the end of
the corresponding caption. You can find out more about these and objects in all areas
of the British Museum's collection by visiting the Museum website: britishmuseum.org/
research/search_the_collection_database.aspx

Frontispiece Cereals were the Greek goddess Demeter's gift to humanity. Triptolemus
acts as messenger, and Demeter's daughter Kore offers a libation of wine as he sets out.
Athenian *krater* (wine-mixing bowl), *c.*470 BC. Terracotta, H. 36.8 cm; diam. 35.7 cm.
J. Paul Getty Museum, Los Angeles, 89.AE.73.

CONTENTS

PREFACE

We have tried to do something quite new in this book. Many people have written about the Roman cookery text *Apicius*, but no one has yet gathered a collection of recipes from the entire ancient world – from both Greek and Roman writings – and shown how they can be recreated in the modern kitchen. We have set the resulting 'menus' beside pictures and narratives of dining, drinking and festivity, which have survived from that period. The result should, we hope, help to bridge the gap between modern experience and the tastes, smells, sights and sounds of two thousand years ago.

This book is a collaboration, but the reader may like to know that the 'I' who speaks about the finding and adapting of ancient recipes is Sally, while the translations and the historical background are Andrew's work.

Sally thanks the many people who tasted her experimental recipes and contributed through their advice to the final form of the book. Their honesty and frankness were invaluable in creating recipes that were both authentic and pleasurable to eat. Special thanks are due to Professor Barrie Hall and Annabel Hall, Terry McKay, Philip Hunter, Pete Whitby, Angela Dicks and Dr Chris Grocock.

Andrew thanks Jane Rowlandson and Gerald and Valerie Mars for their help, and Maureen, Elizabeth and Rachel for unending patience and support. The extracts from Philoxenus and Hippolochus quoted in chapters 2 and 4 are revised from translations by him first published in *Petits Propos Culinaires* nos 26 and 29, with the generous permission of the editor, the late Alan Davidson.

Other translations have been newly made. They are far from literal, sometimes adding a word or phrase to make the meaning clearer, sometimes abridging. Where quantities are given in ancient recipes, 'pint' has been adopted in translation as the rough equivalent of Latin *sextarius*.

1 | The riches of the sea. In this floor mosaic, from a dining room (*triclinium*) at Populonia in Roman Italy, diners saw the living creatures whose flesh they were tasting. Tuscany, *c*.100. 88.9 cm x 104.1 cm. British Museum, 1989,0322.1.

2 | A silver bowl of eggs, a silver ewer, and three wild birds, just killed, waiting to be plucked and roasted. From a series of wall paintings of fine foods in the House of Julia Felix, Pompeii, Italy. Roman, 1st century AD, Museo Archeologico Nazionale, Naples, Italy.

INTRODUCTION

When there is happiness among all the people; when feasters in the house, sitting in rows, can listen to a singer, while beside them tables are full of bread and meat, and a waiter brings wine from brimming bowls and fills their cups: this seems to me in my heart to be the best of all.

(Odysseus to his host Alcinous in Homer, *Odyssey* 9)

The daily life of classical Greece and Rome, although separated from us by two thousand years of history, can be recreated in almost photographic detail.

On the painted cups and wine-mixing bowls of ancient Athens, vignettes of rowdy feasting and of everyday household activity are interspersed with scenes from the legends of gods and heroes. The wall paintings and even the graffiti of Pompeii, buried in the terrible eruption of Vesuvius in AD 79, allow us to see the citizens and slaves of the Roman Empire as clearly as they saw one another. From the garrisons of northern Britain to the fertile valley of the Nile, personal letters of unknown Greeks and Romans, retrieved by archaeologists, bring their writers back to life. And some of the greatest writings of the classical world were copied and recopied by scribes through medieval times. Never forgotten, they have become models of clear thinking and vivid narrative for modern authors.

3 | Celebration in a vineyard. Three
young men, wearing aromatic
wreaths, recline attended by
musicians, one of whom burns
incense. Wine-cups await them
on three-legged tables. Red-figure
pottery *Dinos* (wine-bowl), Italy,
mid-4th century BC. H. 76.5 cm.
British Museum, 1856,1226.4,
bequeathed by Sir William Temple.

These precious clues to the ancient world are not as easy to interpret as they seem. Not only were there huge contrasts between rich and poor; there was the divide between slave and free. The documents give us the chance to hear the voices, and see through the eyes, of all of these, yet it is not easy to put ourselves in their place.

One way in which we can attempt this is through the realities of every day. In any society, food and drink are at the centre of social life. A wealth of information is available on what Greeks and Romans ate and drank – in pictures, in written texts, in archaeological finds. In this book, therefore, we place real ancient recipes beside descriptions of household life and festivity from different times and places around the ancient Mediterranean.

Each of our eight chapters is based closely on Greek or Latin texts, supported by archaeological evidence. The narrative texts we use begin about 700 BC with the *Odyssey*, the compelling Greek epic of the wanderings of Odysseus. Our last major source is a conversation manual, written about AD 200 for Romans studying Greek: luckily for us, this little-known textbook runs through the dialogue needed for a leisurely visit to the baths finishing up with a hot supper (and with tips to the cook and waiters). Thus each chapter in turn takes a different kind of social grouping, a different occasion. Together they suggest the true variety of Greek and Roman life and food.

Immediately after this introduction you will find help with the problems of recreating ancient food, along with notes about some unfamiliar ingredients. At the end of the book are guides to further reading, including translations (where they exist) of the ancient texts from which our recipes come.

When the *Odyssey*, one of the two masterpieces of Greek storytelling, was composed, Greece was a land of isolated farmsteads and small towns, beset by wars and piracy. There were no big states: each little town had its protecting wall, and each country farm had its thorn hedge. The magic of the *Odyssey* is that its hero views this world as an outsider, for Odysseus is a shipwrecked wanderer, a beggar. If we can approach the world of early Greece at all, how better than to do it through his eyes?

Greece produced barley for bread, olives for the irreplaceable olive oil, grapes for abundant wine. But in that rocky landscape many Greeks depended on the sea for much of their food. Fishermen and seamen by necessity, they were beginning to explore the wide Mediterranean, the 'wine-dark sea'. In the centuries to come they would spread out and build new Greek towns all round the Mediterranean, at hundreds of sites that offered a natural harbour, a stretch of farmland, a route for inland trade.

Greek towns grew into cities, with the spectacular temples, theatres and monuments that are still to be seen, but somehow they held on to their independence. Cradles of local democracy, they led the world for a time in science, philosophy, seamanship and warfare. Sea trade brought the luxuries that were tasted at Greek *symposia* or drinking-parties (see chapter 2), where serious discussion alternated with music, games and acrobatic displays. Food and wine, the gluttony of fellow citizens and the self-importance of cooks were continual themes of comedy at annual drama festivals.

By 350 BC, when the gourmet Archestratus (see chapter 3) was searching the markets of the Mediterranean, Greek cities dotted the coastline from Spain and France all the way to the Near East. Greeks of Marseilles were enjoying the wines of the Rhone valley, Greeks of Libya were exporting precious silphium resin to the kitchens of their homeland, Greeks of the Black Sea were pickling tuna. But they were losing their independence to the powerful kingdoms that now began to emerge. Archestratus himself, a Sicilian Greek, was a subject of the tyrannical kings of Syracuse.

Macedonia soon became the dominant power. It was from tiny Macedonia that Alexander the Great (356–323 BC) set out on his amazing career of conquest. Soon master of the old Persian Empire, he took Greek settlers and the Greek way of life to the Middle East and beyond, and brought back the marvellous wealth

4 | Alexander the Great. Alexander's Eastern conquests brought new foods to the Greek world. Silver *tetradrachm* issued after his death by Lysimachus, one of his bodyguards, who had proclaimed himself king. Lampsacus, Thrace (now Turkey), *c*.305–281 BC. British Museum, 1919,0820.1.

5 | Fishermen hauling in their catch. Embossed red-slip, from the region of Carthage in Roman North Africa, c. AD 400. Diam. 17.8 cm. J. Paul Getty Museum, Los Angeles, 81.AE.40.1.

of the East. These riches, spent at lavish feasts such as the wedding of Caranus (chapter 4), caused ruinous inflation and social unrest in Greece after 300 BC. The scientists who went east in Alexander's time brought new foods to Greece: citrus fruits, peaches, pistachio nuts – and even peacocks.

While the Macedonian kingdoms spent their riches, however, Rome's power grew. Between about 400 and 50 BC this country town of central Italy, drawing at first on native resources (as seen in chapter 5), became ruler of all Italy before conquering in turn Spain, Macedonia and Greece, northern Africa, Gaul (France) and the whole eastern Mediterranean. The wealth of the East was transferred westwards, and with the wealth came the demand for new luxuries. Inventive Greek cooks, and novel Greek delicacies, came to Rome. Chapter 6 draws on the hilarious *Satyricon* of Petronius and on other writings of the first century to sketch the heyday of rich and powerful imperial Rome.

The inspiration for chapter 7 is an invitation to a lady's birthday party. Found among discarded documents of the commander's office at one of the Roman garrisons in northern Britain, it combines with other texts to build up a picture of the daily life of soldiers and others in the distant provinces of the great empire. The Romans brought to Britain many of the herbs, vegetables and fruits that now seem native.

With chapter 8 we return to the great capital. In hot and sticky Rome the baths were favourite leisure resorts. In these luxurious establishments one swam, exercised, steamed, was massaged – and then one ate. In this setting we glimpse the food and wine of the later empire, inheritance of medieval Europe.

The life of the very poor saw little change over this long period. Bread was the staple food (barley bread for many Greeks, wheat bread for Romans), and some cities, including Rome itself, issued a free bread ration. Those who could not bake made varieties of porridge or polenta with their wheat and barley. For some there was nothing else to eat but bread, fruit and vegetables gathered from the wild, and such delicacies as shellfish and snails.

Even the leisurely banquets of the rich began with bread, however. For wealthy Greeks of about 400 BC the one main meal of the day started in the early evening (and drinking and talking might go on all night). At a men's dinner-party the host's wife and young children were never seen. Guests' wives were not expected, though some men might bring girl friends. Men reclined on couches, each with a small table; older boys, if lucky enough to be allowed to attend, would sit on a father's or friend's couch. A host would often hire a cook and waiters for the occasion. The room would be lit with hanging lamps. Scents would fill the air, for perfumed oils and wreaths of sweet-smelling leaves would have been passed around. Both wheat and barley loaves were served in baskets. The successive dishes of the main course followed one another in a definite order, taken by a waiter to each diner in turn for him to select a morsel. They

6 Greek wine-strainer, later prized as an antique by a Roman collector. Silver, Greece, 4th century BC. W. 21.6 cm; diam. (of bowl) 10.5 cm. J. Paul Getty Museum, Los Angeles, 96.AM.89.4.

began with appetizing savouries such as fresh fruit, shellfish, roasted birds, salt sturgeon and tuna, and meat delicacies in highly flavoured sauces; they progressed to fine fresh fish, and perhaps climaxed with stewed or spit-roasted lamb or kid.

Then the tables, with discarded scraps and bones, were cleared away and clean tables took their place. With the dessert course, known to both Greeks and Romans as 'second tables', wine was served. Greek hosts always mixed wine with water — it was a host's duty to ensure that his guests did not become too drunk too soon! The dessert consisted of cakes, sweetmeats, cheese, dried fruits and nuts: a wealthy host would demonstrate his generosity with a varied selection of these sweets as well as with a fine choice of wines.

The emphasis now turning to wine, the dinner-party became a drinking-party. Sometimes the host and guests made their own entertainment, ranging from philosophical and literary talk to songs and instrumental music. Or entertainers might be hired, slave musicians, dancers and acrobats. The dinner just described is the archetypal Greek dinner of history and literature. It is not typical of all cities, or of all times. This book will show how Greece and Rome, civilizations of contrasts, introduced endless variety on the theme.

These were not the first cultures in which attention was paid to the ingredients and the special flavours of food and wine. There are recipes on cuneiform tablets from Mesopotamia of the third millennium Spices, herbs and vintage wines were found in the burial chamber of King Tutankhamun of Egypt (c.1346–1327 BC). But so far as we know the Greeks were the first to think seriously about the importance of cookery as one of the skills or arts of human life. Professional cooks, needless to say, were in no doubt about that. Even Plato (427–348 BC), however, gave a few sentences of his philosophical dialogue *Gorgias* to putting cookery in its place. Around the same time an anonymous medical writer likened the work of the cook to that of the musician, in a passage of little-known poetic prose that makes a fine introduction to a collection of ancient recipes.

From the same notes come different tunes: from sharp, from flat; all are notes, but each has a different sound. The most different combine best, the least different combine worst: if one composes all on the same note, there is no pleasure at all. The boldest, the most varied sequences give most pleasure. So it is that cooks make food and drink for us, creating dishes from dissimilars and similars. Now they vary the ingredients, now they use the same ones but with different effect. If one makes all alike, there is no pleasure. If one puts all together in the same dish, it will not be right. The notes of music sound some high, some low. The tongue tastes food as if it were music, distinguishing sweet and sharp, discord and concord, in all that it encounters. When the tongue is attuned there is pleasure in the music; when it is out of tune there is agony!

Recreating Ancient Food

When you begin to experiment with ancient food, people will ask: 'How do you know what it should taste like?' The answer is that no one knows, and no reconstruction is secure. The recipes in this book, therefore, are a personal interpretation of dishes that are as much as 2,500 years old.

Most ancient recipes present a basic list of ingredients with no indication of quantity. The method is often stated in a brief and confused sentence, or left entirely to be inferred. Even more important, there is no hint of what should be the dominant flavour. Fortunately Greek and Latin poets and agricultural writers occasionally provide clues as to how a dish looked or tasted and the manner in which ingredients were prepared and stored. These are invaluable aids to interpreting ancient recipes.

Cooking is an instinctive art. It should never be an absolute science, bound by precise quantities, times and temperatures. The recipes that

7 | Dancing to the music of the double pipe and castanets. Vignette inside an Athenian drinking cup (*kylix*), found at Vulci in Italy. Red-figure pottery, attributed to Epiktetos, Greece, *c*.510 BC. H. 12.2 cm; W. (including handles) 41 cm. British Museum, 1843,1103.9.

follow should not be seen as the only way to prepare each dish – not least because the best ancient cooks shared this instinctive approach to cookery. It is no accident that the major Roman culinary text, the collection of recipes entitled *Apicius*, gives hardly any quantities for ingredients. The book was almost certainly written by cooks for other cooks to use and they would not need to be told precisely what quantities to use: that kind of knowledge is acquired with experience of the spices in use and also the taste of the consumer.

The dominant flavours of Greek and Roman cuisine are honey, vinegar, a fermented fish sauce (of which more later) and a vast array of fresh and dried herbs and spices. The secret is to balance the sweetness with the bitter, sour and unusual flavours that appear in the recipes. The Romans (and to a lesser extent the Greeks) appear to have been unduly fond of sweet flavours in sauces. Honey and grape syrup appear in many. This does not mean, however, that modern recreations of ancient sauces must be cloyingly sweet: sweet is always balanced with sour flavours. Once you have developed a feeling for ancient food, you can imagine yourself, as a slave-cook, introducing a group of northern barbarians or provincials to the delights of this new and unusual cuisine.

Greek and Roman cuisines differ mainly in the quantity of seasonings used. The essential flavours are the same. The Romans are said to have been 'porridge-eating barbarians' before they discovered Greek food towards the end of the third century BC. Eastern cooks, some of them prisoners of war, introduced the Roman elite to the new seasonings and flavours

8 | Preparations for a drinking party: a Roman actor in the role of a cook or slave, laden with a wineskin, an amphora and a basket. Terracotta, Roman Cyprus, c. AD 300. H. 17.8 cm. British Museum, 1903, 1117.1, donated by Sir Robert Hamilton Lang.

of the eastern Mediterranean. In this nouvelle cuisine of 200 BC honey, vinegar, fish sauce, dry and sweet wine, cumin, coriander, oregano and many other herbs were subtly combined to create a simple culinary style that stresses the natural flavours of the fish or meat of the dish. The Romans took to the new cuisine rapidly and developed their own ideas: they developed a more sophisticated and imaginative palate with complex and surprising flavour combinations not to everybody's taste. Newly rich and powerful, they displayed their wealth in their food as spices were costly. They left themselves open to ridicule and parody. A stage cook, in a comedy by Plautus (c.250–184 BC), mocked this new trend:

I don't season a dinner the way the other cooks do. They serve up a whole meadow in their dishes – they treat the guests like grazing cattle, shoving greens at them, then seasoning the greens with more greens. In go fresh coriander, fennel, garlic and alexanders, and on the side there's sorrel, cabbage, beet and blite: they pour a pound of silphium into it, and smash mustard seed in on top: stuff so fierce it makes their own eyes water before they've finished grinding it. When they cook a dinner they aren't flavouring it with seasonings, but with night-owls that are going to eat out your living intestines! No wonder people around here die young when they pack up all this green stuff inside them, vegetables that are frightening even to talk about, let alone eat. If the cows won't eat it, you can be sure that people will!

Classical Greek cuisine could add three or four spices or herbs to a dish while in a typical recipe in *Apicius* as many as ten strong flavourings are to be found. Just as with complex Oriental dishes, the result should be highly appetizing, for each Roman cook had to temper his recipes to the tastes and requirements of those who would share the meal.

Roman food can easily defend itself against any charge of excessive seasoning. The simple unadorned Greek style has its merits, there is no doubt. But there is something unique about Roman food: a taste explosion, reminiscent of Indian food at its best, that will be found new, exotic and exciting. The Roman Empire is often thought of as decadent and extravagant, and the cookery book provides some evidence for this, but it also strongly reflects a more refined, tasteful cuisine, a cuisine for the sophisticated, cultured Roman who had as much contempt as any satirical poet for the fashion-conscious gourmets.

Apicius contains such dubious delicacies as larks' tongues, sterile sows' wombs, dormice; a plethora of birds, warblers, parrots, turtle doves, peacocks, flamingoes; sea food such as sea urchins, porpoises, jellyfish. Other sources mention camel hoof and cockerel combs. They are all delightfully exotic and suit the stereotype of the decadent Roman gourmet who chose the most bizarre of foods because they were rare and expensive and fashionable, quite forgetting about the taste. By contrast we have concentrated in this book on foods that are available in northern Europe, are not too expensive, and are worth the attention of a modern cook.

These recipes deserve to be used and are intended to be used. They represent a selection of the best that Greek and Roman cooks have bequeathed us.

The Ancient Kitchen

Our understanding of the ancient kitchen is largely based on evidence from the town houses in Pompeii. Its dominant feature is the hearth, which in more primitive cultures was at ground level but later became a raised platform of masonry at a convenient height. In many of the houses the platform extends from wall to wall, supported by arches for storage of fuel. These arches have often been interpreted as ovens but it is clear that the oven was a separate structure, also at eye level.

The key to this raised platform is that charcoal, without excessive fumes, was used indoors. A gridiron was placed over the coals to take the cooking pots. I have been experimenting with authentic cooking vessels for many years now and the efficiency and versatility of charcoal for cooking is still quite surprising. In fact the simple barbecue of modern fashion utilizes only a fraction of the potential heat generated from a charcoal fire. Vessels could be placed directly in the embers as well as over the heat but the effect is always one of relatively gentle and slow cooking. If a fierce boil of meat or pulses was required it seems likely that well seasoned fire wood was also used, even if this generated smoke within the kitchen.

9 | A peacock perched on a balcony rail. Peacocks, native to India, were kept in Roman gardens; peacock meat and peahens' eggs were costly delicacies. Wall painting from a villa destroyed by the eruption of Vesuvius in AD 79. Plaster and pigment, Roman, c. AD 70. 40 cm x 24.8 cm. J. Paul Getty Museum, Los Angeles, 68.AG.13.

Many of the recipes in this book, which from necessity were prepared in a modern kitchen, have now been reproduced using authentic ceramic pots and metal cooking vessels. Bronze pots have been found in situ in the house of the Vettii in Pompeii, and Roman soldiers have been found buried with their own personal bronze cooking pot. Cheaper earthenware vessels had a shorter life-span and were difficult to keep clean as they were unglazed. In *Apicius* the cook often calls for a new pot, implying that residues from previous dishes could taint some foods. Lead vessels existed, strange as that may seem, and appear to have been used when boiling down must (grape juice) into syrups for sweetening and colouring. Pliny the Elder actually tells us that they liked the particular flavour imparted by lead!

Roman ovens were dome-shaped and could be built into an outer wall. Larger ovens could be free-standing, made of brick and shaped like a beehive. Those found at Pompeii are elaborate structures that could hold many loaves at once. Ovens inside the kitchen were charcoal-fired and either free-standing or used on top of the hearth. The literary sources refer to this type of oven as either *testum* or *clibanus*. They were dome-shaped with a small hole in the top and a projecting flange that seems to have been used to hold the coals, and they were made of bronze, iron or a coarse earthenware.

10 | Mortar for grinding herbs and spices; made at Verulamium (St Albans) in Britain, soon after the Roman conquest, and stamped by the maker Sollus. Earthenware, 1st century AD. Diam. 29.7 cm. British Museum, 1973,0702.16.

A bronze skillet, the handle decorated with vine fronds, modelled with dolphins and other marine creatures, and signed by the maker Boduogenus. Roman, Gaul or Britain. Diam. 16.5 cm. British Museum, 1893,0618.14.

Archaeological finds show that large amounts of grog (sand, stone and broken pot) were mixed with the clay to enable it to withstand the thermal shock of direct contact with the fire.

In use the *testum* is suspended over the fire until very hot, and then the hearth is cleaned. The bread or cake was placed directly on the hearth and the *testum* placed over it. Hot coals were heaped around and on top of the *testum* before the baking process began. Using equipment based on archaeological finds, I have found that a baking temperature of 375–400°F (190–200°C) is easily maintained, which has produced some very successful bread and cakes. It is apparent that these ovens were used in a domestic context for baking honey cheesecakes (pages 110–11), which are best served warm. The accumulated hot ashes from a day's cooking are the ideal medium for the baking process, whereby no heat at all is wasted.

Placed on top of a dish of similar material, *testa* could be used for cooking moist dishes such as meat or fish. The dish would stand directly on the hearth, with the *testum* over the food, and the coals would be pushed up against the sides and on the flange just as for baking. Apicius gives instructions for just such a method when he tells the reader to cook kidneys in a *clibanus*: see the recipe for Barley Rolls (page 64) for a discussion on alternative baking covers. Some very sophisticated pieces of equipment have been unearthed at Pompeii. It seems the Roman cook had access to such items as fish kettles, moulds in the shape of suckling pigs and hare, and portable braziers that could cook and keep dishes hot in the dining room. Other kitchen furniture include fixed stone pillars which served as the base for a wooden table and kitchen sinks, often supplied with hot water. In a larger kitchen an amphora stood against the wall to store wine and fish sauce. The ubiquitous *mortarium* served as the all purpose mixing and grinding bowl. It was a large shallow vessel with grit embedded in the clay to aid the break-up of spices (I own a number of replicas for use in my experiments, and they are far superior to the modern deep smooth mortar, which by comparison is very inadequate). A mortar is essential for reproducing Greek and Roman food. Pounding and pureeing would have been a task for a menial household slave in an ancient kitchen and would have taken hours of effort. If you do not have a slave to hand, then I suggest you invest in a food processor at once!

12 | Roman glass: a collection of tableware found at Gariannonum in Roman Britain (Burgh Castle near Great Yarmouth), one of the string of forts built to guard the 'Saxon Shore' in the 4th century AD. H. (of tallest jug) 12.7 cm. British Museum, 2003,0303.1–11.

Fish Sauce 'Here is lordly *garum*, a costly gift, made from the
first blood of a still-gasping mackerel' – Martial's verse, written to
accompany a little present of a jar of *garum*, cannot change the
fact that Greek and Roman fish sauces have a rather unattractive
sound. Since the *Classical Cookbook* first appeared in 1996 I have
been experimenting with the manufacturing processes involved in
fish sauce production. There is much confusion about the identity
and quality of the various kinds of sauce. My research has been
published elsewhere (see Further Reading) and has concluded that
the *garum* sauce described by Martial, made from blood and viscera
of very fresh fish, was almost certainly a table condiment, sometimes
handled by the diner and used in relatively small amounts over
already cooked food. The other more commonplace kind of sauce
was called *liquamen* and was used in the kitchen by the cook to add
salt and other more complex flavours to most dishes, just as we
would add salt during cooking. *Liquamen* was made using various
kinds of whole small fish such as anchovy, sardine, mackerel, sprat
and herring (any fish too large were cut up) which were then mixed
with salt and left to dissolve and ferment for up to three months. The
resulting liquefied fish was removed from its bone and shipped all

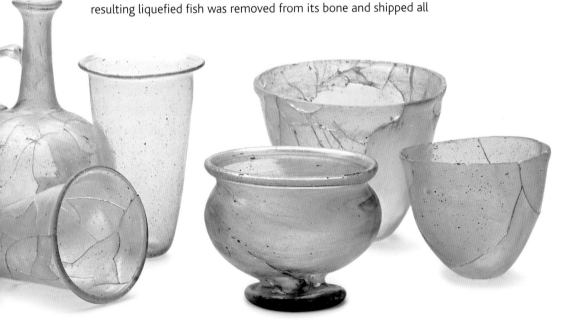

over the Mediterranean in special amphorae. This whole-fish sauce is very similar to the Thai fish sauces so popular today and they serve as a very adequate substitute. Roman fish sauce was nothing like modern anchovy paste: using the latter has been the downfall of many an attempt to recreate ancient recipes.

Fish sauce was manufactured at factory sites along the Spanish and North African coast and these were typically beside a beach or harbour. The fish was only a few hours from the net when the process began. It is now clear that the image of these sauces as a rotten decaying substance is quite misleading. What took place was not bacterial putrefaction (which would have been impossible given the high proportion of salt) but enzymic proteolysis, a process in which the enzymes in the viscera of the fish convert the solid protein into a liquid form. The viscera are therefore essential to the process; without them the protein does not dissolve. The runny fish paste residue left behind when the sauce was strained was called *allec* and was a food in its own right often given to slaves, when of fine quality valued by the gourmet but also a potential fish sauce concentrate that could be reconstituted. According to an ancient encyclopedia, *allec* was applied to burns, but it was effective only when patients did not know what was being used on them. Considering the powerful smell of all these substances, how could they fail to guess?

When setting out to recreate ancient flavours, then, you must start with a bottle of fish sauce. Vietnamese *nuoc mam* or Thai *nam pla* can be bought in any Chinese supermarket. If you cannot find a local source, ask for advice from the nearest Thai or Vietnamese restaurant. It is also necessary to dilute modern fish sauce a little so that it corresponds to the salt levels in ancient fish sauces. Take a 1 lt. carton of grape juice and reduce it by half, cool it and blend fish sauce with boiled grape juice. Use this in all the recipes.

Silphium and asafoetida Silphium was a remarkable spice, known to Greeks and Romans for its medicinal properties as well as for its use in food. It was grown only in Cyrenaica (modern Libya) and was so valuable that the Roman state treasury stored it alongside gold and silver. Then came a disaster for the history of cuisine. The Roman encyclopaedist Pliny (AD 24–79) explains that silphium was no longer to be found:

13 | A Roman bowl with a lid (tureen) from the treasure found at Mildenhall,
Suffolk, England, in 1942. The lid is topped by a figure of Titan; the frieze shows
a mythological battle of centaurs and lions. Silver, Roman Britain, 4th century BC.
H. 19 cm; diam. 23 cm. British Museum, 1946,1007.11–12.

For many years now it has not been seen in Libya: the agents
who lease grazing land, scenting higher profits, had allowed
sheep to overgraze the silphium stands. The single stem found
within living memory was sent to the Emperor Nero. If an
animal should ever come upon a promising shoot, the sign will
be that a sheep after eating it rapidly goes to sleep, whereas a
goat sneezes rather loudly. For a long time now, however, the
only silphium brought to us in Rome has been that originating
in Iran and Armenia, which is plentiful enough, but not nearly
as good as Cyrenaic.

Scholars have found it hard to believe that the silphium of Libya
could really have become extinct, and you sometimes read of its
rediscovery. But the goat never sneezes: the rediscovered 'silphium'
never has the flavour or the power of its legendary forebear. Nero
really did eat the last of it.

Luckily the substitute that was used from Pliny's time onwards, the
'silphium' of Central Asia, is still easily available, although it is

hardly ever used by Western cooks. It is asafoetida, the resin of the plant *Ferula asafoetida*, a relative of fennel. In using this we can be confident that we are doing exactly what the cooks of the Roman Empire, the cooks who first used the recipes of *Apicius*, would have done. Asafoetida is used widely in the Middle East for medicinal purposes, and in India in cookery (it is often listed as an ingredient on packets of ready-made poppadoms and nans). It is rumoured to be one of the secret ingredients in Worcestershire Sauce. The pure aroma and flavour of asafoetida can be compared with leek or garlic, but are best signalled by one of its modern names, 'devil's dung'.

Asafoetida can be purchased in the West as a powder or a tincture both deriving from the resin that is tapped from the root of the plant. The powder is sold as *hing* in Indian food stores and consists of asafoetida resin mixed with flour or bean meal to stabilize it, just as was done with ancient silphium; turmeric may also be added for colour. The tincture is rather more concentrated in flavour and, as *hing* is now readily available, not recommended.

The recipes that follow suggest the quantity of asafoetida to use, whether a pinch of *hing* or one or two drops of tincture. Whichever form you use, take care. Asafoetida can impart a particularly unpleasant taste when used to excess, as I found to my cost during

14 | A wild ibex – a close relative of the domesticated goat – modelled as a silver-gilt pepper pot. Roman, c. AD 390. Part of the Hoxne hoard, found in Suffolk in 1992. H. 6.2 cm; L. 6.2 cm. British Museum, 1994,0408.35.

my early experiments. For a Roman banquet for seventy people, I made half a gallon of lentil stew which I unfortunately seasoned with rather too much asafoetida. In an attempt to salvage the stew I added honey. This worked, but it needed too much honey. As a last resort I added sugar, which saved the dish and turned it into a success. Sugar was a costly rarity in ancient Rome – a medicine, not a food ingredient – but my situation was desperate!

Lovage This, *Levisticum officinale*, is the single most common spice used in *Apicius*. In the first edition of the *Classical Cookbook* I believed lovage leaves were the intended ingredient but I am now convinced that the seed is the right spice to use and consequently I have changed the recipes that call for this. There are at least fifty recipes that begin with the words 'pound pepper and lovage'. It has a bitter sharp flavour that has perhaps caused it to lose popularity in recent centuries, yet it is very useful in everyday cooking, and especially good in fish and pulse (legume) dishes. Its flavour is fundamental to authentic Roman food.

Lovage grows well in a temperate climate so if you have a herb garden, give it a try – but remember that it can reach 10 ft (3 m) tall. The seed is not readily available: so-called lovage seed is usually *ajwain*, an Indian spice which, though similar, is not identical. *Ajwain* will, however, serve as a substitute and can be readily purchased on the web.

Rue Another culinary herb that was once very popular, *Ruta graveolens* is now rarely used. This is a pity: its unusual bitter flavour is still valuable in the kitchen, and it has had a great reputation as a medicinal herb. For safety, as with some other herbs and spices, it should be used in small amounts: it then imparts a necessary bitterness to sweet and rich food and is well worth experimenting with. Rue is a hardy evergreen that grows well in any soil. It is so easily grown – even on the window sill – that its rarity as a culinary herb need not be insurmountable. The stems and leaves of rue can cause an allergic reaction in sensitive skins if picked in bright sunlight, so take care over this.

Other herbs and spices The vast majority of herbs and spices mentioned in this book are readily available from herbalists, health-food shops and supermarkets (aniseed, fennel seed, pine kernels, poppy seed). Most of the herbs can be grown in any garden (pennyroyal, for example). Calamint is not so easy to find, unless you know where it grows wild. Bay berries can be picked in late autumn if you have a bay tree, or they can be purchased on the web. Bitter almonds found in a Chinese supermarket, though not the same species as ancient bitter almonds, are a safer substitute for them, because the bitter variety of our Western almond is poisonous unless roasted.

A good mail-order source of unusual herbs and spices in the UK is G. Baldwin & Co. Ltd, 171–173 Walworth Road, London SE17 IRW.

Passum (raisin wine) 'A Knossos vine, out of Minoan Crete, sends you this raisin wine. It is the poor man's usual *Mulsum*,' wrote Martial. The Romans used many different types of sweetener in their sauces, one of the finest of which was *passum*. Raisin wine was made in Crete throughout ancient and medieval times, and is still produced in Italy and France. It is certainly not a poor man's drink. The poet Martial's little gift-verse, quoted above, is displaying false modesty. For more on *mulsum*, incidentally, see the recipe for Spiced Wine on page 124.

Pliny describes how the Cretans made their famous raisin wine:

Some make passum from any sweet, early-ripening, white grapes, drying the bunches in the sun till little over half their weight remains. Then they gently express the must. The more painstaking makers dry the grapes in this same way, pick the individual grapes and soak them, without the stalks, in fine wine till they swell, and then press them. This style is considered better than any other.

You may be understandably reluctant to buy expensive *passito*, or *vin santo*, modern raisin wine, from an Italian food store, for use as a food flavouring; indeed, you may not be able to find them. A simple dessert wine such as Sauternes will serve very well. However, the Latin farming writer Columella (c. AD 60) gives full instructions for making a version adequate for cooking, based on red wine, which can be imitated on a small scale in the modern kitchen. Take 1 pint (2½ cups/570 ml) red wine and 4 oz (120 g) raisins. Soak the raisins in the wine for two to three days until they are soft and swollen. Blend or

15 | A worshipper of Bacchus: an ecstatic Maenad, carrying a knife and the hindquarters of the kid that she has dismembered. Marble panel, Roman copy of a Greek original, 1st or 2nd century AD. H. 43.2 cm. British Museum, 1805,0703.131.

mash the mixture and strain through a fine sieve, pushing through as much as possible of the pulp. The result can be used immediately.

Defrutum and other concentrated grape juices *Caroenum*, *defrutum* and *sapa* were grape musts reduced by boiling. Like *passum* they were used as sweeteners in sauces. The three names identify different strengths. *Defrutum*, which is needed in some of the recipes in this book, is red grape juice reduced by a half or more. Simply take 1 litre (4⅓ cups) red grape juice, add a few dried figs and reduce it until one third is left, and store. It is used in tablespoon measures.

Ancient and modern cheeses Greeks and Romans made many different types of cheese, but there is little detailed information about them. Most of the recipes simply call for goat's or sheep's cheese (cow's milk cheese is not so often required), without telling us what the texture was. Yet the texture is all-important for the recipes in this book, particularly for the sweet cakes from Cato's farming handbook in chapter 5. Here fresh cheese is essential, because new cheese has little saltiness to interfere with the honey. Ricotta is the best substitute for this cheese.

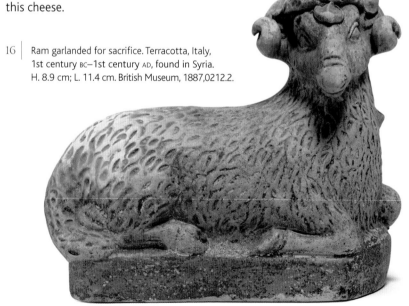

16 | Ram garlanded for sacrifice. Terracotta, Italy,
1st century BC–1st century AD, found in Syria.
H. 8.9 cm; L. 11.4 cm. British Museum, 1887,0212.2.

Columella gives useful instructions for cheese-making. He tells us to put a pennyweight of rennet, the weight of a silver *denarius* (3.99 g), to a pail of milk. The milk is then warmed and, when it begins to curdle, is strained through a wicker basket. It is then moulded and compressed. At this stage it can either be hardened with salt or simply soaked briefly in brine.

I wanted to make a soft sweet cheese to use in the recipe for Layered Cheesecake (page 113), and in following Columella's instructions tried to keep the salt to a minimum. It was also very successful as an eating cheese. Having experimented with many different cheeses, I recommend feta, a type which dates from medieval times and may be made from either sheep's or goat's milk; chèvre, a goat's milk cheese also known as bûcheron, that is sold in the traditional log shape; Pecorino Romano, a hard sheep's cheese very similar to Parmesan; ricotta, which is traditionally made from the whey left over from the manufacture of Pecorino Romano; and Pecorino Toscano, a semi-hard sheep's cheese that is mildly salty and is the closest I can find to the cheese I myself made using Columella's recipe.

A note about brains and sweetbreads Greeks and Romans used these frequently in their stuffings and sausages. They are included in the recipes that follow, but obviously using them is a matter of individual choice. In Britain BSE (bovine spongiform encephalopathy), commonly known as 'mad cow disease', has now been effectively eradicated. Officially lamb's brain and sweetbreads are safe, yet they have become very scarce because of the prevailing caution. An independent butcher may be able to obtain them. Sweetbreads are delicious and it is a great pity that they have become so unpopular. Lamb's brain, as used in Roman stuffing, is also strongly recommended. In the two recipes in which it occurs I have suggested minced (ground) lamb as an alternative.

Measures used in the recipes are level unless otherwise stated.

17 The seductive song of the Sirens. Odysseus has plugged his sailors' ears with wax and they have tied him to the ship's mast. One of a series of wall paintings illustrating the *Odyssey*. Wall painting, Roman Pompeii, before AD 79, probably AD 50–75. 48 cm x 48 cm. British Museum, 1867,0508.1354.

1 THE HOMECOMING OF ODYSSEUS

The ten-year siege of Troy, the victory gained by means of a wooden horse, the unhappy homecomings of the victorious Greek warriors – these stories were familiar to every Greek who went to school. They were told in the *Iliad* and *Odyssey*, two epic tales which, as everyone knew, had been sung by a blind poet, Homer, before recorded history began. They were tales so marvellous that nothing could spoil them, not even the fact that they were set texts to be learnt by heart.

Homer himself did not say how many hundreds of years had passed since Troy fell: he was singing of a lost age of heroes. Now that Troy and Mycenae and Pylos have been excavated we know that if the siege ever happened, as the *Iliad* tells us it did, it must have been before 1200 BC, five centuries or more before the poems were composed.

In the *Iliad* and *Odyssey* a whole world is pictured. It is not the real Mycenaean world of 1300 BC with its labyrinthine palaces and its clay tablets; nor is it quite the Greek world of 700 BC in which Homer must have lived. But it is a world so convincing in every detail, and so familiar to all who read the epics, that it has to be part of any reconstruction of Greek and Roman life.

The *Iliad* tells the story of the Greek warriors' quarrels outside the walls of Troy. There they raided or hunted for meat. And with their roast meat they drank strong, sweet red wine, brought there by seamen who would beach their ships, set up a market on the shore and accept captive slaves and livestock in exchange for their vintage.

In the *Odyssey* we hear of Odysseus' ten-year wanderings and adventures on his way home to Ithaca. He stayed too long, perhaps, with the beautiful goddess Calypso, till Hermes, the gods' messenger, came to tell her that it was time to let him go. The poet shows us Calypso and Odysseus sharing a homely supper before going to bed together for the last time: 'They came to the hollow cave, the goddess and the man together. So he was sitting there on the chair where Hermes had sat, and the young woman laid out every food, for

18 | Roman wine set, including jug, ladle, strainer, stirrer and drinking bowl – once the property of a certain Titus Utius and his daughter. This treasure was found at Arcisate near Como in Lombardy, Italy. Silver, probably made in Campania, Italy, early 1st century BC. British Museum, 1900,0730.6.

him to eat and drink, that mortal men can eat; she was sitting facing godlike Odysseus, and maids put out ambrosia and nectar for her.'

It is part of the charm of the *Odyssey* that a picture of a young housewife, serving her man with food before eating herself, can the next moment be a portrait of a goddess attended by maids – for it was immortals who had to feed on ambrosia and nectar.

Shipwrecked on Scherie (a fantasy island, but believed by many to be Corfu), Odysseus was fortunate to be welcomed to the palace of Alcinous. He paused to admire the king's fruit garden: 'Outside the yard is a big orchard on both sides of the gates, of four acres, and a hedge runs along each side of it. There, tall trees spread their leaves, pears and pomegranates and shiny-fruited apples and sweet figs and leafy olives. Their fruit never fails or falls short, winter or summer, all the year: as the West Wind blows it fertilizes some and ripens others. Pear upon pear grows old and apple upon apple, grapes upon grapes and fig upon fig.'

Food and drink were at the centre of Homeric life. Food left over from the last meal was, by unspoken rule, given generously to a stranger before he was asked his name. And in a king's household, lavish feasting was the order of the day even when the king himself was missing and feared dead.

This, at all events, was what Odysseus discovered when he returned to his homeland of Ithaca. Disguised as a penniless vagrant, carrying a leather begging bag which he hoped to fill with food, drawn by the smell of roast meat (beef, mutton or pork would have been roasted over an open fire in the farmyard), Odysseus stood at last at the doorway of his own smoke-filled hall, watching the carousal of the men who were competing to claim the hand of his faithful Penelope.

At the central fireplace of a Homeric household, we gather, the women, children and servants clustered. Men sat on stools around the walls, each with a well-scrubbed table before him. The tables had to be clean, for the diners had no plates. Joints of roast meat were served, bread was taken around piled high in baskets, a wine-waiter was always at hand. A singer sang stories of gods and heroes – stories just like the *Odyssey* itself, perhaps – and might earn a well-chosen cut of meat in reward for a well-told tale.

This was the scene that the mysterious beggar saw. Soon he was to throw off his disguise, to snatch down the bow that only he could draw, and to massacre the young men who had invaded his house, eaten up his livestock and slept with his slave-girls. Then at last he would taste once more the best wine from his dark storeroom, kept locked away by his old housekeeper to await his return.

There are no recipes in the *Iliad* or *Odyssey*. Yet the poet's vision of the world of the 'heroes' was so sharp and clear that we do hear a good deal of what he imagined they ate and drank. And his imagination ran to simple, hearty, roast meat. The dishes listed below are suggested in one way or another by the epics – and they serve to introduce all the main sources of recipes used in later chapters. Homer might well have been surprised by our selection of dishes, but he would not have been surprised by most of the individual ingredients or the flavours. We cannot suggest a Homeric sweet – except the fresh fruits of Alcinous' orchard, fruits that no one happens to bite into from beginning to end of the epic – but instead we have taken inspiration from Galen's description of a 'pancake', a dish whose history certainly does go back very nearly to the time of Homer.

Now to the wine that would accompany a Homeric feast. The priest Maron, who lived on the north Aegean coast of Greece, presented a fine gift to Odysseus in the course of his travels. Maron 'drew off for me sweet unmixed wine in twelve amphoras, a divine drink: none of the slaves or servants in his house had known it, but himself and his dear wife and one housekeeper only. And whenever he drank the honeyed red wine, filling a cup he poured it into twenty measures of water, and a marvellous sweet smell rose from the mixing bowl.' Some gullible Romans took every word of the epics as history. Pliny writes: 'Fame came earliest, we learn from Homer, to Maronean wine from the Aegean coast of Thrace . . . Homer reported that Maronean was to be mixed with twenty parts of water. In that country the grape retains its strength and formidable power, for a very recent author, Mucianus (three times Consul), reported that when he was there he saw each pint being mixed with eight of water: it was black in colour, fragrant, and became fuller with age.'

We cannot really taste Maron's wine. We only know, from the phrases that came naturally to the poet, that Homeric wine was 'black' (as red wine really is, especially in earthenware cups), 'fiery',

19 | Mistress drinks greedily; slave girl walks gloomily behind, carrying a wineskin on her head. Athenian mug (*skyphos*). Terracotta, *c.*470–460 BC. H. 15.3 cm; W. (with handles) 27.5 cm. J. Paul Getty Museum, Los Angeles, 86.AE.265.

'smoky' and sometimes 'sweet' or 'honeyed' – and that the host mixed it with water before it was served. For an epic feast, there can be no better choice of dry white wine than the firmly aromatic Mantinea, just such a wine as Menelaus' neighbours might have brought in for his sons' wedding feast – or the lighter Robola of Cephallenia, where Odysseus is supposed to have held some land. Choose a powerful red wine: solid Nemea, perhaps, from the venerable vineyards in the hills north of Argos. Wine from here was surely good enough for Agamemnon. As a dessert white wine, there is the gloriously sweet and aromatic muscat of Lemnos, in the north Aegean, just off the Thracian coast. A Greek delicatessen can find all of these, and a Greek mineral water to go beside them. Whatever the heroes might think, we prefer to serve the water separately from the wine!

PORRIDGE (KYKEON)

Fair-haired Hecamede made *kykeon* for them – Hecamede whom the old man had got as his prize from Tenedos, selected for him by the Greeks because of his excellence as an adviser. First she moved a table up to them, a fine polished table with a dark gleaming stand: on it she placed a bronze dish with an onion in it as relish to the drink, and also yellow honey. Next came the heap of holy barley meal. Thus, in a cup, the lovely woman made a *kykeon* for them with Pramnian wine: she grated goat's cheese into it with a bronze grater, and sprinkled barley meal on it, and when she had the *kykeon* she invited them to drink.

Homer, *Iliad* 11, 638–41

What was this curious, nourishing brew that the captive woman prepared for Nestor's friends after a hard day's work at the siege of Troy? Whatever it was, it occurs again and again in early Greek poetry – and the reader soon comes to feel that it has a ritual element. As a mixture of wine and cereal, it brings together the gifts of Dionysus, the wine god, and of Demeter, the goddess who gave us wheat and barley. It could be made dangerously powerful, too. Women who knew about herbs could use a *kykeon* for strange purposes: perhaps to send men to sleep; perhaps worse. Circe 'stirred cheese and barley and yellow honey into Pramnian wine and mixed harmful drugs with this *kykeon*' to turn Odysseus' sailors into swine.

How, then, was *kykeon* made? It may be an impossible quest, but I have at least attempted to rediscover this food of the heroes. The first clue comes from the name itself, for kykân means to churn or clot or thicken by stirring. This suggests something like a soup or even a porridge. A Byzantine scholar made the very same connection: '*Kykeon* seems to have been somewhere between food and drink,' he argued. 'Perhaps really it was something that was supped like soup.'

At first I imagined that the thickening agent was the barley, and that it must stand in the wine until it becomes soft and chewy. But even then it does not truly clot or thicken. Was the barley ground before it was added? If so, it was roasted first, to remove it from its husks. The poet seems to specify 'roasted and ground meal', but even roasted and ground barley will not thicken the mixture. After various experiments I tried placing the wine, barley, honey and a little soft goat's cheese in a pan and heated the mixture. As would be expected, this made a very pleasant porridge.

A recipe in Cato's farming handbook confirmed that I might be getting near to the true nature of *kykeon*. 'Carthaginian porridge to be cooked thus,' he instructs. 'Put 1 lb emmer in water till it is thoroughly soaked. Pour it into a clean vessel. To this add 3 lb new cheese, ½ lb honey, 1 egg. Mix all together well and turn into a new pot.' Emmer, a now rare species of wheat, would have been roasted while still in its husk and then ground by hand, probably to the texture of semolina. Substituting wine for Cato's water and eliminating the egg, which would thicken and enrich the mixture further, we have a very similar dish to *kykeon*.

Things become clearer. The soft new cheese – something like ricotta in texture – is the primary ingredient and the major thickening agent. The barley meal gives structure to the porridge and prevents curdling. The clotting and churning that define *kykeon*, however, are linked to the cheese, not the barley. When cooked out gently, this mixture produces a soft pourable porridge that could indeed be supped from the cup. Cato's recipe is very good as it stands. Divide the quantities by four and use semolina instead of emmer.

When all is said and done, these approaches to *kykeon* are, at best, informed guesses. The truth remains to be discovered: the pleasure in researching ancient cuisine is in the detective work, the hunt for clues that leads to unexpected tastes and textures and, with luck, may lead close to the original recipe.

Serves 4

---

4 oz/120 g/¾ cup semolina
12 oz/375 g ricotta cheese
2 tbsp/60 g honey
A little beaten egg

Place the semolina in just enough water to cover it and allow to soak for 10 to 15 minutes. When soft, drain away any remaining water and add the ricotta cheese, honey and beaten egg. Bring slowly to boiling point, but do not let it boil. Allow to simmer for a few minutes.

OLIVE RELISH

A maid poured water from a beautiful gold jug over the visitors' hands into a silver bowl, and drew up a carved table. An aged housekeeper had put out bread, adding many relishes, and encouraged them to taste all that was in the house. A waiter set out for them bronze trays of all sorts of meats, and gold drinking-cups. A servant often passed by to pour wine for them.

Homer, *Odyssey* 1, 136–43

How to make green, black or mixed olive relish. Remove stones from green, black or mixed olives, then prepare as follows: chop them and add oil, vinegar, coriander, cumin, fennel, rue, mint. Pot them: the oil should cover them. Ready to use.

Cato, *On Agriculture* 119

Cato is the early Roman soldier and politician whose farming handbook forms the basis of chapter 5. This recipe therefore dates from about 200 BC, but olives provided relish and flavouring all through ancient times. The olive tree had been under cultivation in Greece for a thousand years, if not longer, when the *Iliad* and *Odyssey* were composed; classical civilization is almost unimaginable without it. At classical Greek banquets olives were served in brine, and sometimes, no doubt, they were served as relishes similar to this. Olive pastes and relishes are widely available today in delicatessens.

   One or two details of the ancient recipe are unclear. By 'fennel, rue, mint' Cato clearly means the fresh leaves. The recipe works well if the 'coriander', too, is the fresh leaf. But by 'cumin' he must mean seed: the leaf is not aromatic. I find that adding cumin overpowers the herbs, so it is listed as optional below. Fennel leaf will not be easy to find unless you grow it yourself, though that is not difficult: it must be fresh, as the leaf loses its flavour when dried. The distinctive aniseed flavour of fennel leaf is also found in the bulbous root of some modern varieties, which can now be found on sale as a vegetable, so the chopped root will serve as a substitute. To make life easier buy pitted olives – but do buy them loose, from an Italian or Greek delicatessen, not bottled, canned or vacuum-packed.

4 oz/120 g black olives

4 oz/120 g green olives

4 tbsp/60 ml/red wine vinegar

4 tbsp/60 ml olive oil

1 heaped tsp chopped fennel leaf or finely diced fennel root

½ level tsp ground cumin (optional)

2 tsp chopped fresh coriander

2 tsp dried or chopped fresh rue

2 heaped tsp dried or 3 tsp chopped fresh mint

Chop the olives roughly and pour on the vinegar and olive oil. Prepare the herbs, chopping them finely if fresh, and add to the mixture. Place the olive relish in a sealable container and pour a little olive oil over the top. At this stage it can be eaten, as Cato firmly says, but I find that it improves with a few days' marinating. It is so delicious that I have rarely kept it for longer. Try it with pitta bread, accompanied by a sharp sheep's cheese such as feta.

20 | The olive harvest. Trees were said to fruit more steadily if not treated violently – but this was still the usual way. Athenian wine-jar attributed to the Antimenes Painter. Black-figure pottery, Attica, Greece, c.520 BC H. 40.6 cm. British Museum, 1837,0609.42.

TORONAEAN SHARK OR TUNA

In Torone you must buy belly steaks of the porbeagle shark. Sprinkling them with cumin and a little salt you will add nothing else, my friend, unless maybe green olive oil: when they are done you will be serving chopped salad for dressing, and the steaks with it. As you cook all these steaks, a 'crew' for your cooking pot, don't mix in a splash of water with them, or wine vinegar, but just pour on oil by itself and dry cumin and aromatic herbs. Cook over embers, not a fierce fire, and stir frequently to take care that they do not burn.

Archestratus 23

21 | Fish-plate, depicting three roughly sketched sea bass and three limpets. Red-figure pottery, Apulia, Italy, c.340–320 BC. Diam. 13 cm. British Museum, 1856,1226.102, bequeathed by Sir William Temple.

It amused later Greeks, who were enthusiasts for seafood, that Homer's heroes 'never ate a fish' – in spite of the fact that they spent ten years fighting at Troy, where plentiful tuna and many other fine fish were to be found. Meat was in reality a rare luxury for most Greeks, which is probably why the poet put so much emphasis on it. As archaeologists know, fish had already been part of the Greek diet for thousands of years , and no apology is needed for including it in an epic menu. Archestratus' instructions, quoted here, date from about 350 BC, but the method used in a household of Homer's time could well have been identical. Of the ingredients that Archestratus calls for, only cumin was not native to Greece. Even cumin is listed, among other aromatics, on the clay tablets in Linear B script used for keeping accounts in the Mycenaean palaces of the Bronze Age; so it reached Greece at least six hundred years before Homer.

Shark is rarely eaten in Britain except in restaurants – and that is a great pity. It is one of the meatiest of all the Mediterranean fishes, and surprisingly well-flavoured. In the USA the closely related mako has become deservedly more popular. If you can find only frozen (rather than chilled) shark, you may prefer to substitute tuna, which is more readily available chilled. If using frozen shark, ensure that it is thoroughly defrosted and drained: it can hold a great deal of water. We shall see more of the trenchant opinions of the gourmet poet Archestratus in chapter 3. Here he insists, in his usual way, on the one Greek city that produced his chosen dish at its best. Torone was in ancient times the centre of a wine-exporting district on the central peninsula of three-pronged Chalcidice in northern Greece. No wine is exported from quiet Torone beach now, and not many visitors stop there, though the holiday resort of Porto Carras is just 15 miles (24 km) up the coast.

Serves 4

---

4 shark or tuna steaks, each weighing about 4 oz/120 g

3 tbsp/45 ml extra-virgin olive oil

2 tsp ground cumin

2 tsp chopped fresh or dried mixed herbs

1/4 tsp salt

Brush the steaks with olive oil. Combine the cumin, herbs (parsley, oregano, coriander and mint) and salt in one bowl. Press a little of this mixture on both sides of each steak and fry them in a little olive oil for 6 to 8 minutes on each side until they are golden-brown. Serve with a crisp green salad dressed with a tablespoon of olive oil, a tablespoon of red wine vinegar and a splash of fish sauce.

ROAST KID OR LAMB

'Set up a bigger bowl, son of Menoetius, and mix the wine stronger, and make a cup for each of them. These men that have come under my roof are very dear to me,' said Achilles; and Patroclus obeyed his good friend. Then he put down a big chopping-block in the light of the fire, and placed on it the back of a sheep and of a fat goat, and a hog's chine rich in lard. Automedon held the meat for him, and Achilles cut it up. He chopped it and stuck the pieces on skewers. Meanwhile godlike Patroclus made the fire into a great blaze, and then, when the fire had burnt out and the flames had died, he spread the embers and arranged the skewers above the fire, resting them on their supports, and he sprinkled the meat with holy salt. Then when he had roasted it and piled it on trays, Patroclus took bread and set it out on a table in fine baskets, and Achilles served the meat.

Homer, *Iliad* 9, 202–17

Marinated kid or lamb: 1 pint milk, 4 oz honey, 1 oz pepper, a little salt, a little asafoetida. For the sauce: 2 fl oz oil, 2 fl oz fish sauce, 2 fl oz honey, 8 crushed dates, half pint good wine, a little starch.

Apicius 8, 6, 7

Apicius is the well-known Roman cookery book of about AD 400 (see chapter 8). This recipe is one of the few in the book that gives quantities. They seem accurate – at least, they work very well – and I have left them unaltered. The fact that quantities are given has suggested to some scholars that this was originally a Greek recipe. Perhaps more telling is that there are fewer herbs and spices in this dish than in other *Apicius* recipes. Even though it comes from a text a thousand years later than Homer – and even though pepper and asafoetida would have been unfamiliar to the epic poet – the recipe is not out of place in this chapter. It is particularly good with kid if you can find it. I managed to obtain some at a halal butcher in London. It will probably need to be ordered in advance, but repays the extra effort.

Shoulder of kid or 2¹/₂ lb/
1.25 kg leg of lamb

Olive oil

Marinade

1 pint/570 ml/2¹/₂ cups milk

4 oz/120 g/¹/₂ cup clear
honey

1 tbsp/30 g pepper

Salt

¹/₂ tsp asafoetida powder or
5 drops asafoetida tincture

Sauce

8 crushed fresh or dried dates

10 fl oz/280 ml/1¹/₄ cups
red wine

4 tbsp/60 ml olive oil

2 tbsp/60 g clear honey

4 tbsp/60 ml fish sauce

A little cornflour (cornstarch)

Combine the marinade ingredients and leave the meat overnight in the marinade, turning it occasionally to ensure full absorption. Soak the fresh or dried dates in a little red wine at the same time. The next day remove the meat from the marinade, pat it dry, and then roast it in an oven pre-heated to 400°F (200°C/gas mark 6), well seasoned and with olive oil. The timing should be 20 minutes to each 1 lb (450 g) and 20 minutes in addition. When the meat is nearly ready, pound the dates to a pulp and add to the remaining red wine, honey, fish sauce and oil. Bring to the boil and cook out briefly, and thicken with cornflour (cornstarch). When the joint is cooked, remove it from the oven and leave to rest for 10 minutes before carving thick slices and serving with a little of the sauce on the side.

22 | A hare (gilt) attacked by a hound: small silver pepper-pot from the Hoxne hoard. Roman Britain, c. AD 390. H. 4 cm; L. 4.2 cm. British Museum, 1994,0408.36.

CHICKEN STUFFED WITH OLIVES

Bird: Put broken fresh olives in the cavity, sew up and boil. Remove the olives when cooked.

Apicius 6, 5, 7

This is one of *Apicius'* simplest recipes, lacking the numerous spices of which so many of his recipes are full. It could have been prepared in almost any ancient household. The principle behind it is that the olives should give the chicken their flavour and then be discarded. This is fine in itself – but what a waste of olives! I therefore use pitted olives and serve them with the meat.

My inclination to experiment with ancient recipes beyond the confines of the text prompted me to try a number of variations on this dish. The peppercorns are my addition: they were available in Roman times, though not in early Greece. The chicken can be roasted instead of boiled, using olive oil with a little fish sauce as the medium. Olive relish (see page 42) can be used to form a stuffing if a small amount of cooked bulgur wheat is added to it – the result is excellent. As for the chicken itself, by Homer's own time the first Greek cocks had probably crowed! The 'barnyard fowl', native to southern China, had gradually spread westwards to Greece: unmistakable vignettes of cocks and hens can be found in Greek vase-paintings of about 700 BC. They were exotic Eastern birds. Geese, however, were kept in Homeric farmyards, and were already being carefully fattened with wheat. Duck, goose, quail and pigeon would also be appropriate substitutes in this recipe.

Serves 2–4

6 oz/170 g black olives, preferably pitted 1 small fresh chicken 2 bay leaves Salt 10 black peppercorns 1 onion 1 carrot 1 celery stalk	Chop the olives roughly and stuff the chicken with them. Using a large darning needle, sew up the cavity with cotton thread or fine cooking string. Place the chicken in a saucepan and cover with water. Add the bay leaf, salt, peppercorns and vegetables. Bring to the boil and simmer for 1½ hours until tender. Remove from the water and cool slightly before carving.

23 | Half-filled, this Greek wine-cup became a pool with water-birds patrolling its banks. Terracotta, from the eastern Aegean island of Samos, c.550 BC. W. (with handles) 18.7 cm; diam. 14.3 cm. J. Paul Getty Museum, Los Angeles, 86.AE.57.

PANCAKES WITH HONEY AND SESAME SEEDS

Let us find time to speak of other cakes, the ones made with wheat flour. *Teganitai*, as we call them, are made simply with oil. The oil is put in a frying-pan resting on a smokeless fire, and when it has heated, the wheat flour, mixed with plenty of water, is poured on. Rapidly, as it fries in the oil, it sets and thickens like fresh cheese setting in the baskets. And at this point the cooks turn it, putting the visible side under, next to the pan, and bringing the sufficiently fried side, which was underneath at first, up on to the top, and when the underneath is set they turn it again another two or maybe three times till they think it is all equally cooked. Some mix it with honey, and others again with sea-salt.

Galen, *On the Properties of Foods* 1, 3

It is a continual surprise how little food changes from one millennium to the next. The great physician Galen (AD 129–?199/216), a tireless observer of details of food and drink, gives a description so serious and painstaking that we smile to imagine him making notes as he watched a cook turning pancakes. It is hard to remember that he is writing 1,800 years ago. What is more, the dish was already 800 years old in his time. The early Greek poet Hipponax had written of pancakes 'drugged with sesame seeds'. Comedy gluttons on the Athenian stage had spoken of 'mist rising at dewy daybreak from warm pancakes' and of honey poured over them as they sizzle: a breakfast meal, no doubt, and one that was possibly sold on the streets of ancient Athens from portable braziers.

You can serve modern pancakes with honey and toasted sesame seeds. However, what Galen is describing is not precisely the pancake familiar to us, but something as thick as a blini or even thicker, considering that it is to be turned so many times. I also suspect that more oil was used for frying than we would normally use, and this is reflected in the modern adaptation given opposite.

24 | Equipment for the production of flour and kneading of dough. Illustration by Sue Bird.

4 oz/120 g/1 cup flour
8 fl oz/225 ml/1 cup water
2 tbsp/60 g clear honey
Oil for frying
1 tbsp/15 g toasted
sesame seeds

Mix the flour, water and 1 tablespoon honey together into a batter. Heat 2 tablespoons oil in a frying-pan and pour a quarter of the mixture into the fat. When it has set, turn it two or three times to give an even colour. Cook 3 more pancakes in the same way. Serve all 4 pancakes hot with the remainder of the honey poured over and sprinkled with sesame seeds.

2 THE BANQUET OF PHILOXENUS

The usual picture of the parties and entertainments of classical Athens seems to have room for little more than wine. The word *symposion* meant, simply, 'drinking together'. Those rich enough to have a house with more than one or two rooms would have a room set aside for just this purpose, at least as formal as any English dining-room. It would be furnished with five or more couches around its walls, and its size would be described in precisely this way – a 'five-couch room' or whatever it might be. There would be small, easily portable tables to stand in front of each couch.

There are more details in a unique document from Sicily or Greece of around 400 BC, the strange sensuous *Banquet* of Philoxenus, a poetic celebration of obsessive culinary pleasures, a literary dinner-party:

Water for our hands, a silver jug, a gentle child to pour it;
Goodly sprigs of slender myrtle woven for wreaths.
In came a pair of slaves with a shiny table, and another, and another, until they filled the room.
They fetched in snow-white barley-rolls in baskets,
A casserole – no, bigger than that – call it a *marmite*, full of a

> noble eel with a look of the conger about him,
> Honey-glazed shrimps besides, my love,
> Squid sprinkled with sea-salt,
> Baby birds in flaky pastry,
> And a baked tuna, gods! what a huge one, fresh from the fire
> and the pan and the carving-knife,
> Enough steaks from its tender belly to delight us both as long
> as we might care to stay and munch.

Who was this unusual author? Modern editors assert that it was
Philoxenus of Leucas, a legendary glutton of whom it was said that
he practised drinking unbearably hot water and putting his hand
into the hot water flow at the baths, to train himself to snatch and
swallow the best of each dish as soon as it emerged from the oven.

But, glutton though he was, no one knows if Philoxenus of Leucas
wrote anything at all. It is more likely that the *Banquet* was written
by the once-famous Philoxenus of Cythera, a much more interesting
figure. He was court poet to the ruler of the Greek cities in Sicily,
Dionysius I of Syracuse (*c*.430–367 BC), and was best known for
his tale *Galatea* in which the Cyclops falls in love with a mountain
nymph. The unlucky Philoxenus, rumour said, had once been caught
in bed with another Galatea, the king's mistress, and had been
condemned to hard labour in the Syracusan quarries as
a punishment. There is nothing of this, however, in the *Banquet*!

> At last we had had our fill of food and drink:
> The servants cleared away, and brought in warm water, soap
> and oil of orris to wash our hands.
> They gave us muslin towels, divine perfumes, wreaths of violets.
> Then the same polished tables, loaded up with more good
> things, sailed back to us, 'second tables' as men say:
> Sweet pastry shells,
> Crispy flapjacks,
> Toasted sesame cakes drenched in honey sauce,
> Cheesecake, made with milk and honey, a sweet that was baked
> like a pie;

Cheese-and-sesame sweetmeats fried in hottest oil and rolled in
sesame seeds were passed around . . .

With the bringing in of clean tables came the break between
dinner and drinking-party. At this stage, with the sweets and nuts,
wine was first served; at this point in the evening, wherever they
had eaten, leisured Greeks looked for a house where the wine
promised to flow.

In a respectable house, the dining room was a place for men's
dinners and drinking-parties. Women of the household would be out
of sight, though dancers and flute-girls, hired for the occasion, might
be seen in the dining room often enough.

Entertainment and wine; poetry and music; and often, it seems,
deep and serious conversation. On the occasion that is described
in Plato's famous *Symposium* – how realistically, no one knows –
the philosopher Socrates (c.470–399 BC), the satirical playwright
Aristophanes and their companions debated the nature of love. The
occasion for that famous conversation was simply this: their host,
the poet Agathon, had invited his friends to celebrate his prize at the
annual drama festival of Athens.

Socrates arrived late: typically, he had paused in a neighbouring
doorway to think through a philosophical problem. One or two
uninvited guests had squeezed in meanwhile, but room was still
found for Socrates: the couches were big enough for two guests and
even, at a pinch, for three.

Did they want a flute-girl this time? She had been booked in
advance, but the guests were in favour of conversation, not music.
'I think,' said doctor Eryximachus, 'we should tell the flute-girl to go
away and play to herself – or, if she fancies, to the women indoors.'

And so the discussion began. Aristophanes' fertile imagination
told of the Creator who had taken beings that were originally
spherical and sliced them into two. Some made two men, some
made men and women, some made two women, and all of us are
forever searching for our other halves. When Aristophanes' story was
completed, each of the other participants gave his own ideas on the
theme of love, its origin and its purpose.

The night advanced. A noise was heard in the yard, Plato tells us:

There was a knocking at the outer door, very noisy, as if it were a group of revellers: a flute-girl could be heard.

'Go and see, boys,' said Agathon. 'If it is anyone we like, invite them in. If not, say that we have finished drinking already.' A little later they heard the voice of Alcibiades in the courtyard, very drunk and shouting out, 'Where's Agathon? Take me to Agathon!' He was helped in by the flute-girl and some of his other cronies. He stood at the door crowned with a thick wreath of ivy and violets, with a great many ribbons dangling over his head, and said: 'Greetings, gentlemen. Will you take as fellow-drinker a man who is already very drunk indeed? Or shall we simply put a congratulatory garland on Agathon, our reason for coming, and go away?'

26 | A reclining youth (Pilipos) dismisses a dancer (Kallisto, 'most beautiful'). From an Athenian cup attributed to the painter Brygos. Red-figure pottery, Attica, Greece, c.485 BC. H. (of cup) 32 cm. British Museum, 1848,0619.7.

27 | A party-girl shows her skill at *kottabos*: the last drop of wine was propelled at a target with a clever flick of the wrist. She is using a clumsy basin instead of the expected drinking-cup. Athenian cup, probably by Onesimus. Terracotta, *c*.500 BC. H. (of cup) 8.5 cm; diam. 28 cm. J. Paul Getty Museum, Los Angeles, 82.AE.14.

Alcibiades (*c*.450–404 BC), once Socrates' pupil, now a flamboyant politician but later to be branded a traitor to Athens, was welcomed in. He was installed as the third occupant of Socrates' couch, and the discussion went on, sometimes bantering, sometimes serious. By daybreak, the narrator concludes, most of the guests were asleep – but Socrates was still talking earnestly.

A more down-to-earth author, Xenophon, seems to have felt that Plato had given a false picture of the drinking-parties that Socrates attended. Xenophon's *Symposium* could hardly be more different. The conversation ranged at random over many subjects. There was entertainment, too, brought by an entrepreneur who went from door to door looking for parties. He owned a slave boy who danced and a girl who did acrobatics, leaping in and out of a ring of upturned swords. Socrates' contribution at Xenophon's drinking-party was not to send the entertainers away but to take charge of the programme. He felt that beauty could be displayed to better effect than among swords, and suggested an erotic dance that was performed by the two slaves together.

The recipes that follow will help to build a menu for a classical dinner-party. Several dishes are suggested by Philoxenus' lines just quoted, including the honey-glazed shrimps, the tuna steak and the barley rolls. A further short extract reminds us of some of the 'nibbles' that can be served as the wine continues to flow:

> Fresh young chickpeas in safflower dip,
> Eggs,
> Young soft-skinned almonds,
> Walnuts that children like to chew;
> They served us all the things that are fit to serve at wealthy feasts.
> The drinking, the games of *kottabos*, the clever talk, in which each smart new phrase in turn was greeted with applause,
> All came to an end at last.

Athenians, in the fifth and fourth centuries, enjoyed wines from the Aegean coasts and especially those from the larger islands, Thasos, Lesbos, Chios. The philosopher and scientist Aristotle (c.384–322 BC), who lectured in Athens, was asked on his deathbed to name his successor. The choice lay between Theophrastus (c.371–287 BC) of Eresus on Lesbos and Eudemus of Rhodes. The dying Aristotle sent for Rhodian wine. 'This is truly a sound and pleasant wine,' he said as he sipped it. Then he asked for a cup of Lesbian wine. 'Both are very good indeed,' he said, 'but the Lesbian is the sweeter.' His followers took the gentle hint and appointed Theophrastus to lead the school.

At least one later writer, the physician Galen, thought the wine of Theophrastus' home town Eresus to be the most aromatic and sweetest of all. The wines of these islands are not now often found outside Greece, but the heady muscat of Samos, well known since Byzantine times, will make a fine dessert wine and a stand-in for sweet Lesbian. For a modern representative of Chian, the island where 'black' wine was said to have been invented, we can look a little further afield. Chian vines were transplanted to Italy in Roman times. They could well be ancestors of the Aglianico ('Hellenic') grapes of some southern Italian vineyards. For a good smoky red with Greek ancestry, a fine accompaniment to game and roasts, therefore, choose Aglianico del Vulture.

28 | Mask of the wine god, known as Dionysus to Greeks, Bacchus to Romans, wreathed with grapes. Handle ornament of a Greek or Roman bucket. Bronze, 200–100 BC. H. 21.4 cm. British Museum, 1989,0130.1, purchased with a contribution from the National Heritage Memorial Fund.

HONEY·GLAZED SHRIMPS

This recipe is adapted from various ancient sources: Philoxenus makes the shrimps sound tasty, but his poem does not help in recreating the dish! Fish sauce (for its salt) and olive oil would undoubtedly have been among the ingredients, along with the honey. Oregano is suggested because the Greeks were well aware of its suitability in seafood dishes.

Serves 2

8 oz/225 g large raw peeled shrimps

1 tbsp/15 ml olive oil

2 tbsp/30 ml fish sauce

1 tbsp/30 g clear honey

2 tsp chopped fresh oregano

Black pepper

If using frozen shrimps, ensure that they are well defrosted and drained. Place the oil, fish sauce and honey in a saucepan and add the shrimps. Sauté them gently in the cooking liquor for 2 or 3 minutes until they are tender. Remove with a perforated spoon and keep warm. Continue to cook out the liquor until it has reduced by half. Add the chopped oregano and pour the sauce over the shrimps. Sprinkle with freshly ground black pepper. Serve as a first course with a crusty loaf and a simple salad.

29 | A fish-plate including a cuttlefish as one of its three subjects. Red-figure pottery, Paestum, southern Italy, 4th century BC. Diam. 27.7 cm. British Museum, 1978,0414.54.

TUNA STEAK

This young salted tuna first: it cost two obols. It has to be rinsed very well. Then, seasoning a small casserole, placing the slice in it, pouring white wine over, adding a coating of oil, and then simmering, I shall make it as good as marrow, finally tinselling it generously with silphium.

Alexis 186, quoted in Athenaeus 117d

The original recipe (a snippet from an Athenian comedy) is for *Tarikhos horaion*, which seems to be one-year-old tuna caught 'in season' – that is, on its journey from the Black Sea to the Mediterranean – and then salted, which explains why the cook insists on the fact that the steak should be rinsed to remove unwanted saltiness. This delightful recipe is typical of the Greek preference for preparing food simply and without fuss.

'If you should come to the holy city of Byzantium,' wrote the gourmet Archestratus, 'eat another slice of *horaion* for me there: it is good and tender.' The tuna of Istanbul is, indeed, unbeatable. Nowadays we can buy frozen tuna steaks with little trouble, but it can also be found fresh-chilled at good fishmongers and some supermarkets and is well worth the search.

Serves 2

2 tuna steaks	Use a medium white wine and barely cover
White wine to cover	the steaks: season with salt and pepper and
Salt and pepper	add the olive oil. The steaks can be cooked on
2 tbsp/30 ml olive oil	top of the stove or in the oven and should be
3 drops asafoetida tincture	ready in about 10 minutes, depending on their
	thickness. Before serving add the asafoetida
	tincture to the liquor and reduce a little.

CABBAGE THE
ATHENIAN WAY

Cabbage should be sliced with the sharpest possible iron blade, then washed, drained, and chopped with plenty of coriander and rue. Then sprinkle with honey vinegar and add just a little bit of silphium. Incidentally, you can eat this as a *meze*.

Mnesitheus, quoted in Oribasius, *Medical Collections* 4, 4, 1

Oxymeli [honey vinegar]: Simmer honey till it foams, discard the scum, add enough vinegar to make it neither too sharp nor too sweet, boil again till it is mixed and not raw. For use, mix with water, just as you would mix wine with water.

Galen, *Staying Healthy* 4, 6

This is quite a popular recipe among Greek and Roman writers. Oribasius (fourth century AD), a well-known doctor of the late Roman Empire, has borrowed it from a much older book of dietary advice by Mnesitheus (fourth century BC), a medical writer from Athens. The doctors are interested in this dish because it cured headaches and was good for stomach upsets. At least, that is the claim made by the encyclopaedist Pliny: he gives another version of the recipe, one that he had found in Cato's farming handbook (where it was recommended for stiff joints). It is from the recipe of Cato (c.234–149 BC) that I have borrowed the salt in my modern version.

Whatever its medicinal value, Mnesitheus was quite right about cabbage in honey vinegar being delicious as a starter or side dish. It still is, and is simple to prepare. Romans were enthusiastic growers and eaters of cabbage. Pliny describes three types. The first was a curly one whose leaves were 'like parsley', comparable perhaps to Savoy cabbage. The second had broad leaves that could be seen growing from the stem, like kale or spring cabbage. The third had tight, closely packed leaves and appears to have been a white cabbage. He goes on to outline how many illnesses cabbage could cure. It was used as a poultice for wounds. If taken before a meal it prevented drunkenness, and if taken after drinking it could cure a hangover, but sadly our experience doesn't confirm this!

1 small white cabbage

2 heaped tsp chopped fresh green coriander in oil

2 tsp chopped fresh or dried rue

2 pinches asafoetida powder

Salt

Honey vinegar

4 oz/120g/¹⁄₂ cup honey

2tbsp/30 ml red wine vinegar

First make the honey vinegar. Follow Galen's advice: boil the honey and skim it, add the vinegar and reduce a little. Store until needed. Finely slice the cabbage; wash and drain it. Toss with the herbs and 3 tablespoons honey vinegar and sprinkle with the asafoetida powder and a little salt.

30 | A greengrocer at his stall. Illustration by Sue Bird.

BARLEY ROLLS

First I shall recall the gifts to humankind of fair-haired Demeter, friend Moschus: take them to your heart. The best one can get, the finest of all, cleanly hulled from good ripe ears, is the barley from the sea-washed breast of famous Eresus in Lesbos – whiter than airborne snow. If the gods eat barley, this is where Hermes goes shopping for it.

Archestratus 4

Among the cereals, barley was the most popular in ancient Greece, as Archestratus' enthusiasm attests, but even there it was not all that often used for bread. In Rome, by contrast, barley was the punishment ration for soldiers. Under the Roman Empire, Greeks too came to despise the grain that grows so well in the Greek climate.

Barley is very low in gluten. When only pure barley meal is used for bread, the resulting loaf is flat and heavy. Its keeping qualities are poor; the crust and texture can be very dry. It seems likely that ancient bakers, if preparing barley rolls for an elaborate banquet such as Philoxenus describes, would have mixed their barley meal with some other flour to produce a lighter loaf: coarse bread would be out of place. Elizabeth David, in her definitive *English Bread and Yeast Cookery*, recommends a 50 per cent mixture of barley meal and strong wholewheat flour, which I have followed. She also quotes a very simple barley bread recipe, originating in Cornwall, that is remarkably well adapted to classical tastes and kitchens and which provides the basis for the recipe given above: 'Cover the newly mixed bread with a cloth and set in a warm place. When risen form into cone-shaped loaves and bake under a kettle on the hearth. The loaves were usually grouped in threes, and the soft crust, where the loaves touched each other, was called kissing crusts.'

Greeks and Romans also baked on the hearth under a cover, or *testum*. Cooks piled red-hot coals over the *testum*, creating a mini-oven on the open hearth. The space inside the oven was moist with steam during baking and this is understood to be very effective in achieving good bread. We cannot really duplicate this technique very effectively at home, though I have found that heating a large casserole or any large metal or crockery bowl that is ovenproof can be effective. Many of the *testa* found by archaeologists have a small number of holes in the top. I have experimented with a large, shallow, clay flowerpot, 12 in (20 cm) across and about 5 in (13 cm) deep. The drainage holes in the top of this allow air circulation. You may have to bake twice if your container is too small to cover all the rolls. All the recipes using these covers work just as well simply baked in the oven.

Makes 12

Leaven

2 oz (¹/₂ cup/60 g) barley flour

1 tsp fresh or ¹/₂ tsp dried yeast

Dough

6 oz (1¹/₂ cups/170 g) strong wholewheat flour

6 oz (1¹/₂ cups/170 g) barley flour

1 tsp salt

For the leaven, dissolve the yeast in 2 tablespoons (15 ml) warm water and use to form a dough with 2 oz (¹/₂ cup/60 g) barley flour. Knead the dough briefly, mould into a pat, cross it lightly and put a thumb-print in the centre. Pour 2 teaspoons warm water into the indentation. Place in a glass dish with a lid and leave to ferment in a warm place for at least 24 hours.

Now for the dough: sift the wholewheat and barley flours together, add 1 teaspoon salt and the leaven and form a dough with sufficient warm water. Knead well and allow to rest and rise in a bowl, covered with plastic wrap or a plastic bag, in a warm place until it has doubled in size. Divide the dough into 12 pieces and mould them with the palm of your hand into smooth balls. Leave to rise in a warm place, covered with a cloth.

Heat the oven to 400°F (200°C/gas mark 6) and also heat a baking tray and an upturned casserole, shallow clay pot or metal bowl – whatever you decide to use as a 'baking cover'. Brush the tray with a little olive oil and place the rolls in 2 circles of 6, with the edges barely touching. Cover with the upturned container and bake for 15 to 20 minutes until lightly golden and hollow-sounding when tapped.

CHEESE AND SESAME SWEETMEATS

Globi to be made thus: mix cheese and semolina as above; make as many balls as you want. Put fat in a hot copper pan: fry one or two at a time, turning them frequently with a pair of spatulas. When cooked, remove them, coat in honey, sprinkle with poppy-seeds, serve.

Cato, *On Agriculture* 79

The cheese and sesame sweetmeats of Philoxenus were such a tempting idea that I resolved to work out a recipe that would reflect something of the ancient flavour. A recipe in Cato's farming manual forms the basis, yet his recipe is anything but complete. 'As above' seems to send the reader back to Cato's recipe for Layered Cheesecake (see page 113); in that recipe, however, the cheese and semolina are separate components.

Some enlightened guesswork is needed to fill the gaps in the Roman instructions. What follows, then, is one way to recreate the cheese and sesame sweetmeats of Philoxenus and Cato. I prefer to use not lard but olive oil as a deep-frying medium – it was certainly more popular among the Greeks and Romans themselves.

31 | Children cooking. Red-figure pottery, Attica, Greece, *c.*425–400 BC. H. 9 cm. British Museum, 1869,0614.2.

Makes about 15

10 fl oz (1¼ cups/280 ml) milk

2 oz (2 tbsp/60 g) semolina

3 tbsp (90 g) honey

4 oz (120 g) ricotta cheese

3 oz (¾ cup 85 g) sesame seeds, lightly roasted

Olive or vegetable oil for deep-frying

Bring the milk to the boil and sprinkle the semolina over it, stirring all the time. Cook out briefly, taking care not to let it burn. Turn into a clean bowl and allow to cool slightly, stirring occasionally. This should give a firm paste. When it is cooler, add I tablespoon honey and the ricotta. Mix well and stir in 2 oz (2 tablespoons/60 g) of the roasted sesame seeds.

Prepare a simple deep-fryer in a saucepan using olive or vegetable oil. Test the oil for temperature by dropping a little of the mixture in the oil: when it rises and begins to colour, the oil is ready. Form quenelles using 2 teaspoons: take a small amount of mixture in one spoon, cup the other spoon around it and pull it off; repeat the action until you have a smooth egg-shaped ball. Drop 2 or 3 sweetmeats at a time into the hot fat and turn them occasionally until they are golden-brown. Lift from the oil and drain on paper towels. Cook the rest of the sweetmeats in the same way. Warm the remaining honey and toss the cooked sweetmeats in it, then toss in the remaining roasted sesame seeds. These sweetmeats are delicious eaten either hot or cold.

3 THE MARKETS OF THE MEDITERRANEAN

The Mediterranean world in which the Greek cities flourished – and
fought one another – was at least as open to travel and trade as it
is now. It was a world of ominous political changes. In that, also, it
resembles the present day.

The Greeks had founded cities in much of Sicily, in southern Italy
and along the Mediterranean coasts of what is now France and
Spain. The African coast, however, had been colonized by Phoenicians
from Syria. Their new metropolis, Carthage, dominated the southern
seaways and continually disputed possession of Sicily with the Greek
monarchs of Syracuse. Phoenicia itself now provided a Mediterranean
fleet for the great Persian Empire, which had threatened to conquer
Greece and was often involved behind the scenes in petty wars
between Greek cities. Meanwhile, on the northern shores of the
Aegean, the power of the kings of Macedon, the wily Perdiccas (died
413 BC) and his successors, was growing.

It took five months to sail from southern Spain to the eastern end
of the Black Sea. Five months was almost a whole sailing season,

for long-distance voyages in winter were avoided. Shipwrecks were enough of a risk even in summer.

These long sea routes were busy with merchantmen, with fishing boats, and often with pirate vessels and warships. Trade was a risky and complicated business: almost every city had its own currency, its own laws and market regulations, its shortages and surpluses. Even so, there were many who invested in trade, and some who became rich. A city such as Athens had grown prosperous on the trade of the Aegean and the Mediterranean, in spite of Spartan rivalry, in spite of Macedonian and Thracian threats. In a scrap of Athenian comedy we can read a kind of hymn, satirical yet truthful, to the wealth that came to Athens by sea:

> Tell me now, Muses, how many good things the god Dionysus brings us in his black ship as he plies the wine-dark sea. From Cyrene, silphium and oxhide; from the Hellespont, mackerel and every salt fish; from Thessaly, porridge and ox ribs; from King Sitalces, an itch for the Spartans; from King Perdiccas, many a shipload of lies. The Syracusans send us pigs and cheese; as for the people of Corfu, may the sea-god Poseidon damn them in their slick ships, for they have shifty thoughts! Incense from Syria; fair Crete provides cypress-wood for sacrifices; Africa has ivory for sale; Rhodes has dreamy raisins and figs. From Euboea come pears and fat apples; slaves from Phrygia; mercenaries from Arcadia. The Paphlagonians send us the chestnuts and glossy almonds which are the ornaments of any feast. Phoenicia provides wheat and the fruit of the date-palm; Carthage sends rugs and fancy pillows.

Trading laws and regulations were often inscribed on stone to be appealed to by either side in a dispute. On one of these inscriptions we can read that the citizens of the prosperous island of Thasos tried to control local trade in wine: 'Must nor wine, the fruit on the vine shall not be bought before the New Moon of Plynteria: any offending buyer shall pay a fine, stater for stater ... No Thasian ship shall land foreign wine between Mount Athos and Cape Pacheia, or it shall pay the same penalty as for serving water for wine, and the pilot shall pay the same ...

There was trade in many other commodities besides food and wine. Athens reached a wide market with the fine painted pottery that provides some of the illustrations in this book. Slaves, including people who were kidnapped by pirates or captured in war, were bought and sold. Other people travelled voluntarily to find a living – including cooks, for Syrian bakers and Sicilian cooks were already widely sought after.

However, food was certainly the centre of interest at many harbour markets of the ancient Mediterranean. In one comedy after another, on the Athenian stage, hosts and cooks boasted of the fish they had found at market. We know something more of the quality and variety of market produce in those times thanks to a most unusual writer of about 350 BC.

Archestratus was a Sicilian who 'circumnavigated the world to satisfy his hunger – and even lower appetites', said a Roman scholar: quite unfairly, because to judge by his surviving poetry Archestratus wrote only about food! He must certainly have been an inveterate traveller. How else could he have found out about the specialities of all these small seaside cities, well over fifty of them, from Sicily to the Black Sea? Most of them hardly get into the history books; yet what Archestratus says of them rings true, and their specialities are sometimes exactly the same now as they were 2,400 years ago.

Archestratus had no time for fancy dinner-parties or complicated food: 'All to dine at one hospitable table,' he wrote; 'there shall be three or four friends altogether or at most five, or you would have a tentful of plundering mercenaries.' In writing of food his chief concern, repeated over and over again in different words, was that the true flavour of fresh produce, chosen in the right place at the right time of year, should be allowed to come through and not be covered up with layers of spices and strong seasonings. We gave one recipe from Archestratus in chapter 1, and in chapter 2 we quoted him on the barley of Lesbos. Here, now, is a typical recipe of his:

In autumn, as the Pleiades go down, you can cook bonito – and you can cook it in any way you please. Why should I spell the methods out for you? You could not spoil it if you tried. But if you want to be told this too, friend Moschus: the very best way for you to deal with this fish is to use fig leaves and fresh oregano (not very much), no cheese, no nonsense. Just wrap it up nicely in fig leaves fastened above with string, then hide it under hot ashes, keeping a watch on the time when it will be baked. Don't overcook it. Get it from beautiful Byzantium, if you want it to be good: and if you have it from somewhere near there, it will be respectable. The further from the Dardanelles, the worse it will be!

Archestratus was ready, too, to advise on the choice of bread to eat alongside his recipes: 'Take a Thessalian roll, a circling whirl of dough well kneaded under hand. They call it "crumble" in Thessaly; emmer bread is what others say. I also commend a child of bread-wheat, the bread of Tegea that is baked under ashes. Fair is the loaf that famous Athens sells to mortals in her market-place; those from the clay ovens of vinous Erythrae, white and blooming with the gentle seasons, are a joy with dinner.'

What to drink with the Mediterranean menu set out in this chapter? Archestratus' answer to the question would certainly be: if you have no stores of old wine, drink the best wine available for tasting on the market on the day of your meal. Even in those days, there were too many wines for anyone to be able to judge fairly among all of them. The philosopher Democritus (fifth century BC) alone believed that it was possible to count grape varieties. 'He claimed to know every variety to be found in Greece. Others have pronounced them uncountable and infinite,' said Pliny.

Archestratus himself (like Aristotle!) preferred the taste of Lesbian wine, but he also praised the aroma of the Phoenician wine that came from Byblos. This was not too different, perhaps, from the 'wine of Helbon' that Persian emperors drank and that the prophet Ezekiel saw exported from Tyre. As a modern stand-in for the red wine that Archestratus might have drunk we can take the remarkable Château Musar of Lebanon. Otherwise, for this chapter, it is appropriate to look to Sicily and to suggest wines from what was not only a very early site of Greek colonization but also one of the earliest homes of Greek gastronomy. There is the heavy red Corvo, the widely marketed table wine of Archestratus' native island. Fish dishes, however, usually call for white wine. Here Sicily can offer white Corvo – or you might find a lighter Sicilian white made from the Grecanico grape that, from its name, ought to have something Greek in its ancestry. Fine sweet whites, apart from the well-known Marsala (an eighteenth-century invention), come from the small islands off Sicily. Moscato di Pantelleria and Malvasia delle Lipari both bear names that link them with Byzantine Greece. Muscat was the favourite of many a medieval traveller to Constantinople. Malvasia, or Malmsey as the variety is known in English, is named after the trading port of Monemvasia.

33 | Silver wine-jar with lion and griffin handles. Persia, late 4th century BC – the last years before the conquest by Alexander the Great. H. (with handles) 27 cm; diam. (mouth) 11.3 cm. J. Paul Getty Museum, Los Angeles, 86.AM.751.

34 | A catch of dolphin-fish (*Coryphaena hippurus*, now also known as mahi-mahi). Wall-painting from Akrotiri, the town destroyed by the eruption of Thera, Santorini, Greece *c.*1630 BC. National Archaeological Museum, Athens, Greece.

ROCK EEL WITH MULBERRY SAUCE

A big rock eel was to hand: I baked the middle cuts, and I'll poach what's left over and make a mulberry sauce.

Sotades Comicus, quoted by Athenaeus 293a–d

Obedient to the comedy cook's instruction to make a mulberry sauce I have developed a recipe that combines elements of the sauces prescribed for fish in both Greek and Roman texts. Mulberries are a tree fruit similar in appearance to blackberries. They have a very short season and, unless you have a mulberry tree, are hard to find. I use blackberries: they serve well unless you are lucky enough to obtain the real thing.

The fish referred to here have many names: smoothhound and rough hound, huss, dogfish, rock salmon, rock eel. Under one name or another they are readily available from fishmongers. They are not really eels or salmon but relatives of the shark, though smaller and not so dangerous! Some do grow to around 5 ft (1.5 m) long: their prey is crabs and lobsters. The flesh is pink, firm and delicately flavoured. In Britain rock eel is a fish-and-chip-shop fish, usually eaten in batter, though it deserves better.

Serves 4

---

8 oz (225 g) blackberries
(or mulberries if available)

5 fl oz (²/₃ cup/150 ml) red wine

4 rock eel steaks

5 fl oz (²/₃ cup/150 ml) white wine

Bouquet garni of oregano and rue

2 tbsp (60 g) honey

2 tbsp (30 ml) fish sauce

1 tbsp (15 ml) vinegar

3 drops asafoetida tincture or
½ tsp asafoetida powder

A little cornflour (cornstarch)

Wash and pick over the fruit and place it with the red wine in a saucepan to heat. Poach the fish steaks in the white wine with the bouquet garni. Remove the fish and keep warm. Add the white wine and the bouquet to the fruit and cook out for 10 to 15 minutes. Add the honey, fish sauce, vinegar and asafoetida. Pass the sauce through a strainer: push the pulp through, leaving the seeds. Return to the heat and thicken with a little cornflour. Serve the fish steaks with a little sauce poured over one edge.

BREAM IN CHEESE AND OIL

Bake bream at seaside Carthage: first rinse it well. You will see a good big one at Byzantium too, with a body the size of a round shield. Deal with it whole, thus: when you have taken it and coated it well all over with cheese and oil, hang it in a hot clay oven and then bake it through. Sprinkle with cumin-rubbed salt and grey-green oil, drenching it generously with the divine liquid.

Archestratus 13

This is a delicious combination of tastes. The pungent sheep's cheese and delicate flavour of the fish meld very well. However, there are practical difficulties in duplicating Archestratus' method. It proves impossible to generate the fierce temperatures of a clay oven in a domestic setting, and without this heat the dish cannot be precisely recreated. Under the fiercest temperatures possible in a modern oven the cheese melts and falls off and makes an awful mess of the oven! After experiments with various cheeses I settled on Pecorino Romano, which is similar to Parmesan in texture and is the most stable under intense heat. The method that Archestratus recommends, if we could follow it, would allow the cheese to 'set' as a crust around the fish, sealing in the juices. In *The Classical Cookbook* I have attempted to recreate this texture while baking the fish conventionally.

Archestratus specifies *sparos*, annular bream, a species that tends to be on the small side. Greeks and Romans knew well over a dozen different kinds of bream, many of them corresponding better with what the recipe seems to say about the size of the fish. Evidently larger bream could be substituted, but they are difficult to obtain and the smaller are actually ideal for this adaptation. In North America, the bream family (*Sparidae*) is represented by the porgy. Choose a small variety to recreate this recipe.

35 | Fish-plate depicting cuttlefish, sea bass and electric ray. Red-figure pottery, Campania, Italy, c.350–330 BC. Diam. 24.7 cm. British Museum, 1876,1112.1.

1 sea bream or porgy, weighing about 3 lb (1.5 kg)

8 oz (225 g) Pecorino Romano cheese

3 tbsp (45 ml) olive oil

1 tsp salt

1 tsp ground cumin

Clean and carefully descale the fish, remove the fins and take off the head. Break up the cheese and put it in a food processor with the oil. (It can be pounded in a mortar if you have no food processor.) Process for a few minutes until you have a smooth, firm paste. Brush a non-stick baking tray with olive oil or line it with baking parchment and lay the fish on this. Spread half the cheese mixture over the fish, ensuring that the skin is completely hidden by the cheese. Carefully turn over the fish and repeat. Heat the oven to 425°F (220°C/ gas mark 7) and bake the fish for 10 minutes. Take it out of the oven, carefully turn it over and return for a further 10 to 15 minutes maximum. Mix the salt and cumin together and sprinkle it over the crust. Finish with a tablespoon of olive oil dribbled over the fish.

SALT MEAT STEW

Salt meat or slices of gammon (fresh meat similarly). Salt meats are first boiled by themselves to remove saltiness. Then all goes into a casserole: four parts wine, two parts must, one part vinegar, coriander seed, thyme, anise, fennel all roasted and put in at the beginning. Simmer. When half done, add honey and a bit of cumin (some also add pepper) and, putting the stew into a warm serving-vessel, add bits of warm bread.

Oxyrhynchus cookery book (see also p. 93)

This is a simple yet appetizing stew, a peasant meal with the addition of more spices than would be available to most peasants. It is recorded in a Greek papyrus from Egypt but it could equally have been a Roman dish: the ingredients are reminiscent of sauces found in *Apicius*.

Traditionally pork was salted not because of a flavour preference, but as the most economic way to preserve it for the winter: excess saltiness was then removed by the initial boiling specified in this recipe. Salted pork would hang in the fireplace in many ancient households.

Most of the flavourings listed are seeds, and we are not unfamiliar with roasting these, but why roast the herb thyme? The answer is simply that when thyme is dry-roasted the green leaves are easily removed from the stalk, making the herb easier to use.

I lb (450 g) gammon joint
or smoked ham

1 pint (2½ cups/570 ml)
white wine

10 fl oz (1¼ cups/280 ml)
white grape juice

5 fl oz (⅔ cup/150 ml)
white wine vinegar

2 tsp coriander seeds

1 tsp aniseed

1 tsp fennel seeds

6 small sprigs of thyme

1 tsp ground cumin

1 tbsp (30 g) honey

½ tsp coarsely ground
black pepper

2 thick slices coarse
wholewheat bread

Cut the meat into small chunks, cover with water in a pan and bring to the boil. Discard the water, pour the wine, grape juice and vinegar over the meat and return to the heat. Combine the whole spice seeds and the thyme, spread on a baking tray and dry-roast them for 5 minutes in the oven at 400°F (200°C/gas mark 6). Shred the leaves from the stems of the thyme and place them in a mortar along with the seeds. Pound them until they are like breadcrumbs. Add this mixture to the stew and continue to simmer. Cook the stew for a total of 45 minutes. Towards the end add the cumin, honey and pepper. Cut the bread into chunks and place them in the oven for 5 minutes to dry them out a little. Add the bread to the stew: it will eventually soak up and thicken the juices.

36 | Pig garlanded for sacrifice, thereafter to be butchered and eaten. Bronze figurine, Roman Italy, 1st century BC–1st century AD. H. 2.5 cm. British Museum, 1824,0414.1, bequeathed by Richard Payne Knight.

FISH IN CORIANDER CRUST

Prepare the fish carefully, put in a mortar salt and coriander seed, crush finely, roll the fish in it, put in a baking dish, cover, seal, bake in the bread-oven. When cooked remove, season with very sharp vinegar and serve.

Apicius 10, 1, 4

This ancient equivalent of fish in breadcrumbs is remarkably good, and the method is suitable for many kinds of white fish. Do not forget (as I once did) to sprinkle it with vinegar before serving: it is dry and unpalatable without this final touch.

Serves 2

2 tablespoons (30 g) coriander seeds

1 tsp salt

2 fillets of cod, haddock or plaice

White wine vinegar

Roast the coriander seeds in a dry frying pan for a few minutes. Cool slightly, then pound with the salt in a mortar until you have a well-broken mixture. Pat the fish fillets dry with kitchen paper and feel along the back for and remove any small bones. Roll the fillets in the mixture as if it were breadcrumbs, then place them in an oiled casserole and cover with a lid. Place in the oven and cook for 15 to 20 minutes. Serve immediately, sprinkled with a good white wine vinegar.

37 | Red mullet, sea bass, electric ray, sargue (a species of bream) and cuttle-fish. Not to scale – red mullet is a small fish, but good; electric ray is big and not very interesting to eat. Red-figure pottery fish-plate, Campania, Italy, c.360–330 BC. Diam. 24 cm. British Museum, 1872,0603.1, donated by Gaston Feuardent.

DELIAN SWEETS

'On Hecate's Island,' says Semus in *Deliad* II, 'the Delians sacrifice what they call *basyniai* to Iris, goddess of the dawn. It is wheat dough, boiled, with honey and the so-called *kokkora* (which are a dried fig and three walnuts).'

Athenaeus 645b

Another sweet: Take durum wheat flour and cook it in hot water so that it forms a very hard paste, then spread it on a plate. When cold cut it up up in lozenges, and fry in best oil. Lift out, pour honey over, sprinkle with pepper and serve.

Apicius 7, 11, 6

The first recipe is sketchy and difficult to interpret. Were the dried fig and the walnuts ingredients in *basyniai*, or were they a separate offering to the goddess? I believe that they were separate – so I offer them to guests beside my Delian Sweets in order to remain loyal to the text. How were the sweets themselves made? The Greek word here translated 'boiled' could also mean 'fried', which does not help. But the second recipe, quoted from *Apicius*, sheds light on a possible method. This gives something remarkably like choux paste, though without the enriching eggs and fat. In creating a modern version, therefore, I have kept choux paste in mind.

   Pepper was once very common as a seasoning for sweets. It is surprisingly good with honey. In our own tradition nutmeg has replaced pepper in dessert and sweet cookery, but nutmeg was practically unknown to the classical Greeks and Romans.

6 fl oz (¾ cup/170 ml) water

2 oz (½ cup/60 g) plain (all-purpose) flour

Olive oil for deep-frying

2 tbsp (60 g) honey

Poppy seeds or freshly ground black pepper

Bring the water to the boil and add the sifted flour. Beat vigorously as if you were making choux paste. Cook out for a few minutes and turn out on to a large plate, or a marble slab if you have one. Allow to cool completely. Heat the olive oil in a deep-fryer. Cut the paste into cubes: it will be firm but still a little sticky. Test the oil for temperature with a little of the mixture: if it rises and colours, the oil is ready. Drop the cubes in the oil, 2 or 3 at a time. Cook for 3 to 4 minutes until golden-brown and lift out on to kitchen paper. While they are still warm, dribble warmed honey over the fritters and sprinkle them with either poppy seeds or freshly ground pepper.

38 | Preparing Thetis for her wedding with
Peleus: the child of this marriage would
be Achilles. In this detail we see two of her
attendant Nereids; a round mirror hangs
on the wall. Scene from an Athenian *pyxis*
(lidded box), attributed to The Eretria
Painter. Gilded red-figure pottery,
Attica, Greece, c.425 BC. H. 11.4 cm.
British Museum, 1874,0512.1.

4 A WEDDING
FEAST IN MACEDON

Thanks to the skill and determination of Philip (c. 382–336 BC), and
the boundless ambition and energy of his son Alexander the Great,
Macedon grew in two generations from a backward kingdom on the
northern fringes of Greece to a world empire.

Alexander died suddenly, in his palace in Babylon, in 323. More
than almost any other individual, he had changed the course of
history. What was once the monolithic Persian Empire became,
after Alexander, a group of Macedonian and Greek kingdoms
stretching as far east as Afghanistan and the Indus Valley. In Egypt,
under its Macedonian dynasty, the literature of early Greece was
systematically collected, became the subject of sustained and serious
research, and was thus transmitted to Rome and later Europe. In
Greek-ruled northern India the *Conversations of King Menander* with
the philosopher Nagasena (second century BC) one of the great
classics of Pali literature, would help to form the philosophy of
Buddhism. Meanwhile the Greek language and Hellenistic art and
literature of the new kingdoms had a lasting influence of their own,
on the later Near East and on the nascent culture of Rome. Greek
would become the language of the New Testament, the first language

39 | A Bacchic scene: Pan plays on his pipes; a nymph accompanies; Ariadne is seen in the distance. Small silver platter, one of the masterpieces of the Mildenhall treasure. Roman Britain, 4th century AD. Diam. 18.5 cm. British Museum, 1946,1007.2.

of the new religion of Christianity. Without Alexander, the culture of much of the modern world would be vastly different.

From the point of view of Greece itself, Alexander's conquests brought immense wealth, new ideas – and new foods. Aristotle, Alexander's tutor, had encouraged him to take botanists and other scientists on his long journeys. The results, in terms of newly discovered fruits and vegetables, are recorded in the so-called *History of Plants* by Aristotle's successor, the scientist Theophrastus of Eresus. The Greeks who settled in Syria and Egypt experimented with new varieties of their own favourite food plants. The cooking skills of the East were ever more sought after in wealthy households: at the same time the cooking traditions of Greece spread eastwards.

We can begin to visualize the mixture of Greek, Macedonian and Near Eastern cultures that was taking place in the years after Alexander's death through an unusual narrative of about 300 BC that leads us into an aristocratic Macedonian household at the moment of a wedding feast. Hippolochus, an Athenian, was one of the guests: his letter to Lynceus of Samos, describing the festivities, survives in the *Deipnosophists* of Athenaeus. Hippolochus and Lynceus, incidentally, were both students of Theophrastus.

'Twenty was the number of men invited,' Athenaeus tells us. We must take it that the women, even at this wedding feast, were celebrating separately! Each guest on arrival was given a silver drinking-cup – which, when he had drained it of wine, he was supposed to keep. Then, served on bronze plates, came flat loaves on which guests could heap morsels of chicken, duck and pigeon; then a second course, served on silver plates, with geese, hares and kids; and a third, with wood-pigeons, doves and partridges.

We gave the slaves a share of this course, too [Athenaeus now quotes Hippolochus]; and when we had had enough eating we rinsed our hands. Lots of wreaths of all sorts of flowers were brought in, and gold circlets for all.

We were already far from sober when in rushed flute-girls and singers and some Rhodian harp-girls, I seem to think they were naked, only some have been saying they had tunics on. They did their act and went away. Then more girls trooped in each carrying a pair of half-pint flasks of perfume, one silver, one gold, yoked together with a golden strap, which they proffered to each of us.

Next was served something more like a treasure than a dinner! It was a silver dish (with quite a broad gold rim) big enough to take a whole roast porker, and a very large one too, which lay there on its back displaying all the good things its carcass was full of. Baked together inside it were thrushes and warblers, and yolk of egg poured over them. Barbecued oysters and scallops were served next, with a plate for each. After this we had a drink, and each of us was given a stewed kid on a silver dish, with gold spoons.

At last the second tables came in and fruit and nuts were offered to all in ivory baskets, and all sorts of cakes, Cretan and your very own Samian, my dear Lynceus, and Attic, with the receptacle proper to each.

The feast that Caranus, the bridegroom, had arranged for his friends was very different from anything that would have been seen in Greece in earlier times. The distribution of wreaths and perfumes was, admittedly, a Greek custom. But the quantities of food seem vast. There was far too much for any one person to eat. Yet it was not all wasted. Macedonian feasting enabled the guests to display their generosity to slaves and attendants and to take food home for their households. They were even given baskets to carry off the leftovers. And all the plates and utensils, gold, silver and bronze, were given to the guests to take away. Gift-giving was the method by which Macedonian kings had asserted their status and conducted their diplomacy. This, perhaps more than any other feature of the wedding feast, was a local custom, one that had no doubt suffered inflation thanks to the immense riches that Macedonians had now won in the East.

The recipes that follow are linked in one way or another with Macedon and its conquests. One of them comes from the Greek cookery book of which fragments were found among the papyri of Oxyrhynchus, in Egypt, where so much lost Greek literature has come to light. For the kid stew, the main course of the feast described by Hippolochus, we have substituted roast hare, a fine delicacy for a smaller-scale dinner and one of Greece's luxuries (for a recipe for roast kid or lamb, see page 46). The few surviving recipes for ancient Greek cakes and pastries include one of Cretan origin – Hippolochus actually mentions Cretan cakes – and one from Alexandria, the new Greek metropolis of Egypt that still bears the name of its founder Alexander.

If we can judge by Caranus' feast, Macedonians did not look far afield for wine: he served Mendaean and Thasian vintages, from the Macedonian mainland and a neighbouring island. But they drank lavishly. Alexander's court was infamous for drunken quarrelling, sometimes fatal. Alexander, people said, had brought on his own death by over-indulgence in wine.

One of the best-known wines of modern Greece comes from Macedonia. The dry red of Naoussa, from the western hills, has a long history: Naoussa was already admired by travellers in the eighteenth century. There are also a red and a white Côtes de Meliton, from an estate south of ancient Torone. These latter wines, a blend of newly planted French and Greek varieties, cannot claim any historical tradition – but that would certainly not have worried Caranus or his guests.

ROAST HARE

Drenched hare: it is first briefly scalded in water, then arranged in a pan. It is to be roasted in oil in the oven, and when nearly done more oil is to be added. Add the following sauce. Pound pepper, savory, onion, rue, celery seed, fish sauce, silphium, wine and a little oil. Turn a few times: let it finish cooking in this sauce.

Apicius 8, 8, 1

The recipe from *Apicius*, described opposite, will probably be preferred by most readers. For a simpler view of the best way to deal with hare we can look back to the instructions of Archestratus: 'There are many ways, many rules for the preparation of hare. This is the best, that you should bring the roast meat in and serve to everyone while they are drinking: hot, simply sprinkled with salt, taking it from the spit while still a little rare. Do not worry if you see the blood seeping from the meat, but eat greedily. To me the other recipes are altogether out of place, gluey sauces, too much cheese, too much oil over, as if one were cooking a cat!'

40 | Successful huntsman and dog. The huntsman carries a fox and a hare. At Athens hare was the typical game animal. Detail from an Athenian cup by the Tleson Painter. Black-figure pottery, Attica, Greece, c.550 BC. H. 13.3 cm. British Museum, 1867,0508.946.

1 saddle of hare

Salt

1 tsp ground black pepper

Olive oil

2 small onions

2 tsp fresh lovage
or celery leaf

1 tsp dried savory

2 tsp chopped fresh
or dried rue

1 tsp celery seed

½ tsp asafoetida powder
or 3 drops asafoetida tincture

10 fl oz (1¼ cups/280 ml)
red wine

2 tbsp (30 ml) fish sauce

Bring a large saucepan of water to the boil and either place the hare in the pan or pour the water over it to scald the meat briefly. Transfer the meat to a roasting tin and season well with salt and pepper and plenty of olive oil. Heat the oven to 375°F (190°C/ gas mark 5) and roast the saddle for a total of 1½ hours.

Meanwhile prepare the sauce. Chop the onions finely and combine them with the other seasonings and the wine, fish sauce and 2 tablespoons (15 ml) olive oil. Remove the hare from the oven after 1 hour's cooking and add the sauce. Return to the oven for another 30 minutes, basting frequently with the sauce. When the meat is cooked, take it from the oven and keep it warm. Turn the sauce into a pan, bring to the boil and reduce slightly. Carve the meat and serve a little of the sauce on the side.

Hare can be found today at a specialist butcher or a market stall (rabbit may be used as an alternative). A whole hare will feed up to 6 people, and it is not usually sold in joints. The saddle is the best part of the animal: this is what you should use for the recipe. Ask your supplier to skin, draw and joint the hare for you; save the legs for another occasion. Hare is a very bloody meat and the process of scalding it in boiling water is useful to clean the meat before roasting.

BAKED MACKEREL

COOK: 'Do you know how to cook horse-mackerel?'

SLAVE: 'I will when you've told me.'

COOK: 'Take out the gills, rinse, cut off the spines all round, split neatly and spread it out flat, whip it good and sound with silphium and cover with cheese, salt and oregano.'

Alexis 138, quoted in Athenaeus 322c–d

Scad or horse-mackerel is not in fact a mackerel at all. It is a member of the *Carangidae* family, other members of which include bluefish and pilot fish. They all live in the warm waters of the Mediterranean; horse-mackerel alone is also found in British waters yet is rarely seen in fishmongers' shops. The fish is distinguished by prominent eyes and a stepped lateral fin. It is usually treated in the same way as mackerel, but is said by at least one authority to be not as good. I prefer to use mackerel for this recipe: it is easily available and well-flavoured.

Serves 2

2 mackerel
½ tsp asafoetida powder
or 3 drops asafoetida tincture
2 sprigs of fresh oregano
8 oz (225 g) chèvre cheese
Salt

Remove the head from the mackerel and clean the fish. Split each fish all the way down its belly and open it out. Break the spine in 2 or 3 places with a heavy knife and lift out the bone. Remove as many of the little bones as you can. Spread it flat, flesh uppermost, in a greased baking dish. Sprinkle with the asafoetida powder or tincture. Chop the oregano roughly and combine with the crumbled cheese. Pack this mixture over the flesh, pressing it down carefully. Heat the oven to 350°F (180°C/gas mark 4) and bake the fish for 15 to 20 minutes until golden-brown and crisp.

LIVER OXYRHYNCHUS

Cut up good liver, marinate in oil with salt, coriander, thyme, silphium, opos, vinegar; grill on a spit at high temperature; serve.

Oxyrhynchus cookery book

Serves 2

8 oz (225 g) lamb's liver

2 tbsp (30 ml) olive oil

2 tbsp (30 ml) red wine vinegar

1 large handful of chopped fresh coriander

2 tsp dried thyme

Generous quantity of salt and pepper

Carefully skin the liver and remove any sinews and blood vessels. Slice thinly and leave to marinate in the other ingredients for 2 to 3 hours or overnight. Line a grill (broiling) pan with cooking foil and place the liver slices on this with a little of the marinade. Grill (broil) at a high heat for 2 to 3 minutes on each side and serve with a little of the juice.

41 | A small *krater* (wine-mixing bowl) with goat-heads as handles, and with a frieze depicting a stand-off between two goats. Black-figure pottery, found at Camirus, Rhodes, Greece, and probably made nearby, early 7th century BC. H. 14.6 cm. British Museum, 1860,0201.16.

ALEXANDRIAN SWEETS

Itria: thin sweetmeats made of sesame and honey.

Athenaeus 646d

Harpocration of Mendes calls the Alexandrian kind of cake a *pankapra*. This is crumbled *itria* boiled with honey; and, when boiled, they are made up into balls, wrapped in thin papyrus to hold them together.

Athenaeus 6486

There are two kinds of *itria*, the better kind called *ryemata* [flowed out] and the poorer called *lagana* ['wafer'].

Galen, *On the Properties of Foods* 1, 4, 1

Itria: presents; nibbles; biscuity shapes.

Hesychius, *Dictionary*

42 | Fruit bowl containing – all modelled in terracotta – pomegranate, apple, fig, almond and small gourd. Rhodes, Greece, mid-5th century BC. H. 9.5 cm. British Museum, 1864,1007.11.

These scraps of ancient writing give an example of the jigsaw puzzle from which Greek and Roman foods sometimes have to be reconstructed. The ancient Greek word *itria* is the origin of Arabic *itriya* and Sicilian and Calabrian *tria*, a kind of pasta. Yet *itria* were some kind of sweetmeat. They are only vaguely defined, but there is just sufficient information to develop a recipe. They could apparently be thin 'flowed-out' biscuits (cookies) made of honey and sesame seeds. The honey was evidently boiled as a first step: it is not so easy to see what processes followed. The recipe following this one is for a more elaborate version of *itria* known as *gastris*. There more detailed instructions specify roasting the nuts before they are mixed with the honey, so there will be no need to add heat a second time. I have used the *gastris* method as a basis for the simpler *itria*. In both the honey is boiled until it almost becomes caramel and sets in the same way as toffee. The boiling time is crucial to the texture of the finished sweet. Both sweets could be either crisp or chewy: we can see them as ancestors of pralines or nougat. I have enriched the *itria* with some nuts, in the belief that, despite lack of evidence, the sweets of ancient Alexandria would have been as diverse as our confectionery is today. You can be more adventurous and add raisins, chopped dates or poppy seeds if you like.

Makes about 20 pieces

4 oz (1 cup/120 g) sesame seeds

3 oz (¾ cup/85 g) chopped mixed nuts (almonds, walnuts, hazelnuts)

6 oz (¾ cup/170 g) clear honey

Roast the sesame seeds and nuts in the oven at 350°F (180°C/gas mark 4) until they take on a little colour. Put the honey in a saucepan and bring to the boil, then skim and continue to simmer gently for 7 minutes. Add the nuts and sesame seeds to the honey while warm and mix well. Grease a shallow baking tray or dish and spread the mixture out on it. Allow to cool until you can handle the mixture and then mould into balls the size of boiled sweets. Wrap in little pieces of paper and serve with fruit and nuts at the end of a meal.

HONEY NUT CAKE

In Crete they make a little cake which they call *gastris*. This is how it is done: sweet almonds, hazelnuts, bitter almonds, poppy seeds: roast them, watching them carefully, and pound well in a clean mortar. After mixing the nuts knead with boiled honey, adding plenty of pepper. It turns black because of the poppy. Flatten out into a square. Now pound some white sesame, work with boiled honey, and stretch two *lagana*, one below and the other above, so that the black is in the middle, and divide into shapes.

Chrysippus of Tyana, quoted by Athenaeus 647f

Bitter almonds are obtainable from Chinese supermarkets. In the US they are banned from sale, but peach or apricot pits may be substituted. All these are poisonous raw, but safe after roasting. In small amounts they add an unusual tang to the recipe. You can find Greek mountain thyme honey in health-food stores and sometimes in supermarkets. Known as *thymeli*, it has a wonderful flavour and (though fairly expensive) adds a special touch to the sweets.

4 oz (1 cup/120 g) nibbed almonds

4 oz (1 cup/120 g) nibbed hazelnuts

1 tbsp (15 g) bitter almonds

2 tbsp (30 g) poppy seeds

6 oz (1½ cups/170 g) sesame seeds

7 tbsp (210 g) clear honey

1 tsp coarsely ground black pepper (this may be reduced if you wish)

Heat the oven to 350°F (180°C/gas mark 4). Combine the nuts and poppy seeds and roast them to give them colour. Roast the sesame seeds briefly, allow them to cool, then pound or process them to a fine texture. Place 3 tablespoons (45 g) of the honey in a small pan, bring to the boil and simmer gently for 7 minutes. Add the pounded sesame seeds and stir well. Allow to cool sufficiently to be touched and turn out on to a greased table or marble slab. Grease your hands and knead until firm but still warm. Divide into 2 equal portions and keep one of these warm on top of the stove. Grease a shallow square baking tray or pan with olive oil, then, using a greased rolling pin, roll out the cooler portion of sesame paste into a thin sheet to fit inside the tray.

Place all the roasted nuts in a food processor with the pepper and process for a minute or two till you have a fine texture. Boil the remaining 4 tablespoons (60 g) honey for 7 minutes in the same way as before, then add the nut mixture and stir well. While still hot, spread this over the sesame layer and level it off. Roll the second layer of sesame paste into a sheet that covers the nuts. Put it in place, leave for an hour to set and without further delay (or it will get too hard) cut into lozenges. Serve with fruit at the end of the meal, or as a sweet at any time.

43 | Bridal gifts taken from her parents' house to her new husband's. Detail of a wedding procession, led by a torch-bearer. Athenian *pyxis* (round container with a lid) attributed to The Marlay Painter. Red-figure pottery, Attica, Greece, mid-5th century BC. H. 17 cm. British Museum, 1920,1221.1.

44 | A shepherd offers grapes to a seated
woman in this Bacchic pastoral.
Roman wall painting, 2nd–3rd century
AD, from the Tomb of the Nasonii
near Rome. This is the finest surviving
fragment of this richly-decorated
interior, excavated in 1678. 65 cm x
85 cm. British Museum, 1883,0505.2.

5 CATO'S FARM

For us Greek literature begins with the two great epic tales of heroes
and their adventures. Roman literature begins in an utterly different
way – with comic plays and a farming handbook.

The first full-length work of prose that happens to survive from
Roman antiquity is a collection of notes jotted down as advice for
someone who was planning to invest in a farm. The topics covered
seem to be the ones that had concerned the writer himself: choosing
a good business, keeping it profitable, managing slave labour.

> Each time the master visits his farm, he will first greet the
> household spirit. Then he should go round the property – that
> very day, if he can; if not that day, the next. As soon as he is clear
> how the business stands, what jobs are finished and what is still to
> be done, next day he must send for the manager . . .
>
> He must aim for best profit: sell oil when it will pay; sell surplus
> wine and grain; sell ageing oxen, less-yielding cows, less-yielding
> sheep; sell wool, hides, old carts, old tools, old slaves, sickly slaves,
> and anything else surplus. The master has to be a selling man, not
> a buying man.

The reader is told when and where to build a new farmhouse and how to equip it for wine and olive oil production. And, as a bonus for all who are interested in ancient food, there is a fascinating long section of recipes. These are not recipes for main dishes: you and your cook must work out your own choices for dinner. They are recipes for preserving meat and vegetables, for making cakes and sweets, for medicinal drinks and for special kinds of wine. They may seem to be a miscellaneous list, but they have something important in common. These are all items that could be made on the farm and kept for long-term use, or indeed sold at the nearest market. They give a unique snapshot of Roman farm economy long before Rome was the ruler of the world. Here is an example: 'How you should preserve lentils: dissolve silphium in vinegar, soak the lentils in the silphium-vinegar, and stand them in the sun. Then rub the lentils with oil, let them dry, and they will keep quite sound.'

This practical-minded author was one of the best-known figures of early Roman history. It is, in fact, quite remarkable that we have such a close insight into the way that an early statesman's mind worked when he was engaged in his own private business. For this was Cato 'the censor', a man of unusual foresight, unusual strictness, and unusual confidence in his own decisions. To later generations Cato was the typical traditional Roman. A fine military commander in Spain, a fine and honest governor of Sardinia, he had eventually been appointed censor back in Rome and, as

45 | A boar led to sacrifice: the ribbon distinguishes it as a sacrificial victim. Roman bronze, originally perhaps part of a harness. 1st or 2nd century BC. H. 10.2 cm. British Museum, 1873,0820.31.

46 | Silver-gilt drinking horn, modelled as a stag, with inlaid glass eyes. Parthia (the Roman Empire's eastern neighbour), c.50 BC–AD 50. H. 27.5 cm; L. 46 cm. J. Paul Getty Museum, Los Angeles, 86.AM.753.

such, had expelled some well-known men from the Roman Senate for lapses in morality: one of them, so it was said, for no other reason than that he had kissed his own wife while someone else was watching, the someone else being their daughter. Cato thinned the order of 'knights' too, Lucius Veturius being expelled because he was too fat to ride a horse. 'How can such a body be useful to the State,' Cato demanded, 'when everything between gullet and genitals has been taken over by stomach?' Cato was also said to have a fierce aversion to the Greek culture that was then invading Rome and sapping the vigour of Roman youth. But in spite of such stories, he comes over in reality as severely practical.

As governor, he insisted, he would not be attended by a crowd of lackeys because it was a waste of the State's resources. As farmer, he would hold on to his olive oil until the price peaked, and he would keep slaves only while they were fit to work. Whatever he thought of the insidious dangers of Greek culture, Cato advised young Romans to learn Greek. Some of the wines for which he gives recipes are imitations of Greek wines. The cakes in his farming handbook have Greek names: they are a Roman version of Greek patisserie. If these wines and cakes would sell in Italian markets, Cato would make sure that his own farm drew some of the profits.

We know very little of Roman meals in Cato's time. As Rome came to dominate Italy, Sicily, Spain and southern France, the Romans certainly did learn to like the luxuries that were available in the old-established Greek cities in those regions. As Rome fought and defeated Carthage, the Carthaginian books on agriculture were officially translated into Latin: it is from one of these that Columella took his recipe for *passum* (raisin wine), mentioned earlier. Soon Romans would begin to make military conquests in the East. Greek slaves, including Greek cooks, would flood the city; Greek comedies, adapted into Latin, would sweep the Roman stage; and Greek ways of life and love would come to seem more natural than home-grown customs. Cato stands at the very beginning of these exciting developments.

Even in Cato's time Greek wine was in fashion in Roman Italy. Why else should he give those complicated recipes for adding sea water to the must to imitate the wine of Cos?

Yet we can see from the firm and practical instructions for the vintage and the wine trade, elsewhere in Cato's handbook, that the wine of Italy was already big business. Two hundred years later the tireless Pliny tried to write the history of Italian vintages. In early times, he decided,

> … no particular variety is famous, but one particular year is. All varieties gave of their best when L. Opimius was Consul, the very same year in which the Tribune C. Gracchus stirred up the people to rebellion and was assassinated. In that year, Rome's six hundred and thirty-third, the weather was ideally sunny – 'ripe', as people say. These Opimian wines have lasted about two hundred years already, though by now they have reduced to something resembling rough honey, evidently the natural state of wine in its old age. They are no longer drinkable by themselves, not even when diluted with water: their formidable maturity has at length turned to bitterness. They are 'medicines' now, used in tiny doses to improve other wines.

This marvellous year for Italian wines was 121 BC. Ancient wines did not usually last as long as two hundred years! As Pliny remarked in a later section of his encyclopaedia: 'No investment gains faster than wine up to its twentieth year, or loses faster after that – unless its price rises.' This may sound like self-contradiction, but the meaning is clear: wine that lasted longer than twenty years was a rarity. With the simple Roman dishes of this chapter, drink young Italian wines.

47 | Two cooks prepare a fine meal with no expense spared. They are gutting a fawn, which will possibly marinade in the wooden trough. Garlic, spices and flavourings await them on a silver dish. A big silver or bronze wine-jar, elaborately modelled, stands nearby. Roman wall painting of the 70s AD, found in the 19th century in the ruins of a villa near Boscoreale, Italy, destroyed in the eruption of Vesuvius. 69.5 cm x 127 cm. J. Paul Getty Museum, Los Angeles, 79.AG.112.

GARLIC CHEESE

First, lightly digging into the ground with his fingers, he pulls up four heads of garlic with their thick leaves; then he picks slim celery-tops and sturdy rue and the thin stems of trembling coriander. With these collected he sits before the fire and sends the slave-girl for a mortar. He splashes a grass-grown bulb with water, and puts it to the hollow mortar. He seasons with grains of salt, and, after the salt, hard cheese is added; then he mixes in the herbs. With the pestle, his right hand works at the fiery garlic, then he crushes all alike in a mixture. His hand circles. Gradually the ingredients lose their individuality; out of the many colours emerges one – neither wholly green (for the white tempers it), nor shining white (since tinted by so many herbs). The work goes on: not jerkily, as before, but more heavily the pestle makes its slow circuits. So he sprinkles in some drops of Athena's olive oil, and adds a little sharp vinegar, and again works his mixture together. Then at length he runs two fingers round the mortar, gathering the whole mixture into a ball, so as to produce the form and name of a finished *moretum*. Meanwhile busy Scybale has baked a loaf. This he takes, after wiping his hands . . .

Moretum 88–120

Not for the faint-hearted, this fiery *moretum* (garlic cheese). If we take the poet's recipe at face value, it may include fifty cloves of garlic: a pretty powerful mixture, but surprisingly good with a fresh warm loaf and a few olives. The farmer has just a small ball of hard cheese in his larder yet the finished garlic cheese is described as firm enough to make a ball itself. The garlic is quite juicy when pounded and this

48 | A slave, preparing a sauce in a mortar, rubs his eyes: onions are no doubt the cause. Terracotta model from Roman Egypt, 2nd century AD. H. 6.5 cm. British Museum, 1926,0930.17.

determines how much cheese is to be used to produce a finished *moretum*. The olive oil and vinegar soften the mixture slightly but do not turn it into a spread.

The poem *Moretum* is sometimes attributed to Virgil, author of Rome's national epic, the *Aeneid*. The extract quoted here deserves to be a very famous one: it actually provides one of the national mottoes of the United States, '*E pluribus unum*' ('Out of the many, one'), a memorable phrase first used of the green herbs and white garlic of a ploughman's lunch! *Moretum* paints a picture of a poor peasant farmer struggling to make his living. The battle to survive is depicted in epic style, like a hero's quest. He is making his morning meal in the cold and damp of the dawn. He struggles to rekindle the fire in his draughty hovel; he strains to grind his meagre supply of wheat into flour, so that his wife can make their flat unleavened bread in the hearth.

Greeks and Romans used a mortar for grinding and mixing sauces. In this case the farmer would have used a large, coarsely made bowl with a grainy texture that helped to break down the ingredients. If you have a food processor, the effort required to produce the dish is minimal. If, on the other hand, you have to grind by hand you will need a large pestle and mortar. You can also gain first-hand experience of the suffering that the Roman farmer endured as he worked: 'Every so often the acrid smell assails his flaring nostrils and the farmer curses his meal, screwing up his face like a monkey. Now and then he wipes his smarting eyes with the back of his hand, swearing at the blameless fumes.'

Serves 6

2 heads (20–25 cloves) garlic	Peel and roughly chop the garlic. Grate the

2 heads (20–25 cloves) garlic

8 oz (225 g) Pecorino Romano cheese

1 large handful of coriander leaves

2 heaped teaspoons chopped fresh celery leaf

1 tsp salt

1 tbsp (15 ml) white wine vinegar

1 tbsp (15 ml) olive oil

Peel and roughly chop the garlic. Grate the cheese. Roughly chop the herbs. If you are grinding by hand, start with the garlic and salt; break it down to a pulp, then add the cheese and herbs. When you have a smooth mixture add the liquids and mix well. Gather the mixture together and chill. If you are using a food processor, add all the solid ingredients and process until the mixture is smooth in texture, then add the liquids. Serve with a crusty loaf as a snack.

LENTILS

Lentils: boil and when they have frothed add leek and coriander leaf. Coriander seed, pennyroyal, asafoetida root, mint and rue; moisten with vinegar, add honey, blend with fish sauce, vinegar, concentrated must, add oil, stir. Adjust as needed. Bind with starch, add green oil on top, season with pepper and serve.

Apicius 5, 2, 3

Serves 6

8 oz (225 g) green
lentils

2 small leeks
(white parts only)

1 large handful of
fresh coriander

2 tsp chopped fresh mint
or 1½ tsp dried mint

I tsp chopped fresh
or dried rue

Ground black pepper

2 tsp ground coriander

2 good pinches asafoetida
powder or 5 drops
asafoetida tincture

2 tbsp (30 ml) red
wine vinegar

1 tbsp (30 g) honey

3 tbsp (45 ml) fish sauce

I tbsp (15 ml) defrutum
(reduced grape juice)

I tbsp (15 ml) olive oil

Soak the lentils in cold water overnight. Next day rinse them well in fresh cold water and place them in a saucepan with enough water barely to cover. Bring to the boil, skim if necessary and simmer gently. Chop the leeks and fresh coriander and add to the lentils. Combine the mint, rue, 1 level teaspoon ground black pepper, the ground coriander and asafoetida and add along with the liquids. Cook out until the lentils are tender. You can thicken the mixture with cornflour if you wish. Transfer to a serving dish and sprinkle with olive oil and pepper.

CELERY PURÉE

Vegetable purée: boil celery in water with soda. Drain and chop finely. In a mortar crush lovage, oregano, onion, wine, fish sauce and oil. Cook in a saucepan and mix in the celery.

Apicius 3, 15, 2

This is excellent as a vegetable accompaniment for many of the meat and fish dishes in this book and can also be made with other vegetables. I have tried it with leek, cabbage and spinach with success. When making it with celery, if you do not have access to fresh lovage you can substitute 1 teaspoon lovage seeds: these can be found in Indian supermarkets. Celery leaf, which would normally work as a replacement for lovage, would be lost in this recipe.

Serves 4

---

1 celery head

1 medium onion

5 fl oz (⅔ cup/150 ml) sweet white wine

2 tbsp (30 ml) fish sauce

1 tbsp (15 ml) olive oil

2 tsp chopped fresh lovage or 1 tsp ground lovage seeds

2 tsp chopped fresh oregano

½ tsp ground black pepper

Chop the celery roughly and wash it carefully. Chop the onion. Place both in a saucepan with water and bring to the boil. Cook until tender and drain. Place the wine, fish sauce and oil in a saucepan and add the herbs and pepper. Cook out gently for a few minutes. Purée the celery in a food processor or pass it through a metal sieve. Add to the sauce; heat together and serve.

49 | Two silver spoons from the Mildenhall treasure. Knives had many uses; forks were not yet invented; spoons are the only Roman implements that fully belong in the category of tableware. Roman Britain, 4th century AD. L. 17.2 cm. British Museum, 1946,1007.34.

SMOKED SAUSAGES (LUCANICAE)

Lucanicae similarly: crush pepper, cumin, savory, rue, parsley, mixed herbs, bay berry, fish sauce, and mix in well-beaten meat, rubbing it well into the mixture. Then, adding fish sauce, whole peppercorns plenty of fat, and pine kernels, stuff into an intestine (pulled as thin as possible) and hang in the smoke.

Apicius 2, 4

Lucanicae were traditionally smoked above the fireplace and not otherwise cooked. This is no longer possible in the home, but we can still give them a smoky flavour before grilling them. If you have an open fireplace, they can be suspended from the mantelpiece for a few hours while you burn wood. Alternatively you can use your barbecue: sprinkle wood chips over the coals and suspend the sausages at least 12 in (30 cm) above the fire for an hour or so. This

50 | A boar hunt: two nude huntsmen attack the boar, while a hound siezes its hind quarters. Detail from a *krater* (vessel for mixing water and wine), attributed to The Andromeda Group. Pottery, Corinth, Greece, c.575–550 BC. H. 30.9 cm. British Museum, 1772,0320.6.

is the most influential of all Roman recipes! The idea was brought back to Rome by soldiers who had served in Lucania, in the 'heel' of Italy, probably around Cato's time. Peppery, spicy, smoked sausages are still made in many parts of the world, from Palestine to Brazil, under names that can be traced back to *Lucanica*. In Brazil, for example, they are called *linguiça*. The main ingredient is sometimes pork, sometimes lamb. Recipes change with time, however, and the modern versions (even the Italian ones) contain few of the original flavourings.

Sausage skins can be bought freshly made from animal gut; synthetic skins are also available. An independent butcher, who makes his own sausages, will be able to help. You will need the chipolata-size skin. There is no need for an elaborate sausage-stuffing machine: a piping bag and a ½-in (1-cm) icing tube are quite adequate.

Serves 6

1 lb (450 g) belly pork, minced (ground)

2 tbsp (30 g) pine kernels

20 black peppercorns

1 tsp chopped fresh or dried rue

2 teaspoons dried savory

1 heaped tsp ground cumin

1 tsp ground black pepper

30 bay berries (if available)

2 tsp chopped fresh parsley

3 tbsp (45 ml) fish sauce

Sausage skins

Combine all the filling ingredients and mix well: use a food processor if available. If you have fresh skins, they will be preserved in salt and will need to be washed. You will need about 6 x 12-in (30-cm) lengths. Tie a knot in the end of each one. Put a ½-in (1-cm) plain tube in a piping bag and half-fill with the mixture; do not put too much in at a time or it will be difficult to squeeze. Take the open end of the skin, pull it over the tube and push it down repeatedly until the majority of the skin sits like a collar half-way down the tube. Grip this with your finger and thumb and slowly release the skin as you squeeze the bag. Stop squeezing well before the skin has run out, leaving 2–3 in (5–7.5 cm) of skin to allow for shrinkage. It will take some practice before you get this procedure right. When you have used up all the meat, twist each length of sausage into 4 even segments. If you are able to smoke them, drape them over a coat-hanger or similar item and suspend in the smoke. Otherwise cut them into individual sausages and grill them under a medium heat.

CHEESECAKE

Libum to be made as follows: 2 lb cheese well crushed in a mortar; when it is well crushed, add in 1 lb bread-wheat flour or, if you want it to be lighter, just half a pound, to be mixed well with the cheese. Add one egg and mix all together well. Make a loaf of this, with leaves under it, and cook slowly in a hot fire under a brick.

Cato, *On Agriculture* 75

Libum means 'cake'. What kind of cake? It is often talked of by Roman poets, but what they say does not always match Cato's recipe. *Libum* was sometimes a sacrificial cake such as was offered to household spirits in the early years of Roman history; it was sometimes a farmhouse cake, served hot; it was sometimes a delicate honeyed cake that was served at the very end of an elaborate Roman dinner. The poet Ovid (43 BC–AD 18), writing of Roman religious festivals, tells us some tantalizing details. He talks of a *libum* infused with clear honey – and he traces the origin of these cakes all the way back to mythology, and to the discovery of honey by the god Bacchus. Perhaps these particular cakes are included in Cato's farming book for religious reasons – to appease the gods, or to ensure the farm's fertility. *Libare*, after all, meant 'to offer to the gods'. All the ancient writers associate *libum* with honey – all except Cato, and he is the only one who actually gives a recipe. His *libum* works perfectly well without honey. Cato's *libum* is a delicious savoury cheesecake, very successful when served hot. The cheese that is used can be quite salty and mature (I used feta) and the resulting texture, with golden-brown crust and soft centre, is similar to that of a modern baked cheesecake.

If, on the other hand, we take it that the proper thing was to add honey, a soft unsalted cheese must be chosen: the combination of salty cheese and honey is unappetizing. Therefore, two recipes are given here. These cheesecakes, either sweet or savoury, can be baked under a *testum*, or baking cover or simply baked in an oven: see Barley Rolls (page 64) for a full explanation.

Serves 2

3 oz (¾ cup, 90 g) plain flour
9 oz (250 g) ricotta cheese
1 egg
2 bay leaves
2 tbsp (60 g) clear honey

Grease a baking tray and place 2 large bay leaves in the centre. Beat the cheese until smooth, add the egg and beat again to incorporate it. Sieve the flour, add 1 tablespoon to the cheese and stir very gently and slowly to incorporate the flour. Add another tablespoonful and repeat. Gather the remaining flour and sprinkle over the mixture and on to the hands before gathering up the soft dough and very gently forming it into a round ball. Do not knead or in any way attempt to blend all the flour fully into the mixture. Place the ball directly onto the bay leaves. You can cover the cake in an earthenware vessel as a substitute *testum* for authenticity or bake it as it is in a hot oven (425°F/200°C/gas mark 7) until golden brown and firm to the touch for 20–25 minutes. Remove from the oven and immediately score the cake across the centre and pour the warmed clear honey into the gap. Serve at once before it begins to cool.

SAVOURY CHEESECAKE

Serves 4

l lb (450 g) feta cheese
4 oz (1 cup/120 g) plain (all-purpose) flour
1 egg
2–3 bay leaves

This is ideally made in a food processor. Break up the feta and place in the bowl. Process for 30 seconds until the mixture is smooth. Add the sifted flour and the egg and process for a few seconds until you have a soft dough. Mould into a loaf and shape into a slightly flattened circle. Score the top with 3 lines that divide the loaf into 6. Heat the oven to 425°F (220°C/gas mark 7). Place 2–3 fresh bay leaves under the loaf, cover with your alternative cover if you choose to use one and bake for 25 to 30 minutes. Serve while still warm as an accompaniment to a first course or to a savoury course.

51 | Two little boys playing with a kid. This Athenian *chous* (water-jug), or one just like it, is visible centre stage on a small three-legged table. Red-figure pottery, Attica, Greece, late 5th century BC. H. 8.5 cm. British Museum, 1929,1016.2.

LAYERED CHEESECAKE

Placenta to be made thus: 2 lb bread-wheat flour to make the base; 4 lb flour and 2 lb semolina to make the layers. Turn the semolina into water. When it is really soft, put it in a clean mortar and drain well; then knead it with your hands, and when it is well worked add the 4 lb flour gradually and make into sheets (*tracta*); arrange them in a basket to dry. When they are dry, rearrange them neatly. In making each sheet, when you have kneaded them, press them with a cloth soaked in oil, wipe them round and damp them. When they are made, heat up your cooking fire and your brick. Then moisten the 2 lb flour and knead it; from this you make a thin base. Put in water 14 lb sheep's cheese, not bitter, quite fresh; let it steep, changing the water three times; take it out and squeeze it gradually dry with the hands; when properly dry put it in a mortar. When all the cheese is properly dried out, in a clean mortar knead it with the hands, breaking it down as much as possible. Then take a clean flour sieve and press the cheese through the sieve into the mortar. Then add 4½ lb good honey and mix it well with the cheese. Then put the base on a clean table which gives a foot of space, with oiled bay leaves under it, and make the *placenta*. First place a single sheet over the whole base, then, one by one, spread the sheets with the cheese and honey mixture from the mortar and add them to the *placenta*, spreading them in such a way that you eventually use all the cheese and honey, and on the top put one more sheet by itself. Then draw up the edges of the base, having previously stoked up the fire. Then place the *placenta*, covered with the hot tile, and put hot coals around and above it. Be sure to cook it well and slowly. Open it to check on it two or threetimes. When it is cooked, remove it and coat in honey. This makes a 1-gallon placenta.

Cato, *On Agriculture* 76

This remarkable cake also comes from Cato's farming book. The name is Greek (and it had nothing to do with the modern meaning of placenta, invented by a seventeenth-century scientist). In Greek the word could often mean a flat cake with a pastry base; goat's milk cheese and honey were among typical ingredients. A Greek comedy included a brisk exchange between a wordy gourmet and a down-to-earth eater:

'The streams of the tawny bee, mixed with the clotted river of bleating she-goats, placed upon a flat receptacle of the virgin daughter of Zeus, delighting in ten thousand delicate veils – or shall simply say cake?'
  'I'm for cake.'

Roman *placenta*, like *libum*, was not only a delicacy for humans but also a sacrificial cake offered on temple altars. The Roman poet Horace tells of a temple slave who ran away because he was sick of honeyed *placenta* and wanted some good plain bread. Cato's Latin *placenta* is a single, very specific and very complicated recipe. It is likely that Cato was confused by the recipe he was copying. The ratio of ingredients doesn't always work: the 2 lb of soaked semolina will not absorb 4 lb of flour to make a dough for the internal layers; and the base dough, when rolled out, will be several feet across! The thickness of the outer covering is crucial: if made to Cato's recipe, it must have been fairly thick or the cake would have been too large to bake. To make a dinner-party *placenta* we had better ignore the ratios he gives and simply follow the method. The following recipe, then, is a small delicate version of Cato's cake that could have graced a Roman banquet.

Serves 6

---

2 oz (⅓ cup/60 g) semolina

6 oz (1½ cups/170 g) plain (all-purpose) flour

12 oz (340 g) ricotta or full-fat cream cheese

3 tbsp (90 g) plus 4 oz (½ cup/100 g) clear honey

Bay leaves

Place the semolina in a bowl with enough cold water just to cover it. Allow to stand for 1 hour. Sift 4 oz (¾ cup/120 g) flour into a bowl and form a dough with about 2 tablespoons (30 ml) cold water. Knead well and allow to rest. Strain the semolina and remove as much of the water as possible; place in a bowl and knead in 2 oz (⅓ cup/ 60 g) flour. Form a dough and leave to rest. Beat the cheese, add 3 tablespoons (90 g) honey and leave to one side. Divide the semolina dough into 6 equal pieces. Roll out and also pull each one into a circle roughly 8 in (20 cm) across. Take a cake tin or ring of that size and cut each circle into a uniform shape and discard the thicker edges. Carefully lay them on a lightly floured table to dry.

When the pastry is dry take the flour and water dough and roll it out with plenty of flour into a circle about 18 in (45 cm) across. Half way through switch to using the back of your hands to pull the dough out. It should resemble strudel paste in thickness.

Now you can begin to build the cake. Grease a large baking tray with olive oil and place 3 or 4 large fresh bay leaves on it. Carefully lift the large flour-dough base on to the baking tray and let it drape over the edge. Place a tablespoon of the cheese/honey mixture on the base and spread it out. Place one layer of the semolina pastry on to this and put another tablespoon of the honey mixture on this. Repeat until you have used up the honey and cheese; finish with a layer of pastry. Your pastry base should have at least 5 in (13 cm) of dough each side of the stack of honey layers. Standing before the cake, pick up the far edge of the base and pull it towards you and place it across the top layer. Move your hand down to the right and pull another part of the edge towards the centre; this will create a fold which you can repeat all round the cake. The final edge needs to be tucked in. Gather the pastry at the top and twist it off, leaving a small knob. Cover with your alternative cover and bake in a pre-heated oven at 425°F (220°C/gas mark 7) for 45 minutes to 1 hour until golden-brown and crisp around the edge. Allow to cool slightly and place in a large dish with a lip. Pour the rest of the warmed honey over the cake and allow it to soak in for 10 minutes. Serve warm.

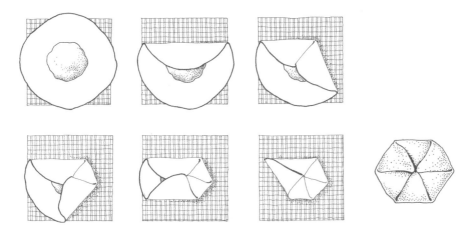

52 | Steps in folding the pastry for the *placenta* (layered cheesecake). Illustrations by Sue Bird.

6 THE WEALTH OF EMPIRE

Cato, old-fashioned puritan though he seemed to many later Romans, marks a continuing trend. In the days of empire, even a moderately well-off Roman liked to talk of his country farm. He would hint at the wonderfully fresh produce that the farm manager and his wife had sent down to Rome that very day, a treat for the master and his dinner guests. The satirical poet Juvenal (born AD 67) pushes the fashion to the edge of ridicule:

Listen to the menu: no market stuff here. A fine plump kid, the most tender of the herd, from my farm at Tivoli, so babyish it has more milk in its veins than blood; wild asparagus gathered by the manager's wife after her spinning; big warm eggs wrapped in straw; and their mothers[!]; and grapes preserved half a year but just as good as when they were fresh; and Signine pears and Syrian pears and apples fresh-scented from their harvest baskets, rivals of the Picentine and nothing for you to fear, cured by the autumn chill of any dangerous roughness in their juice.

54 | An impressionistic landscape vignette, from the wall paintings of the villa (near modern Boscoreale, Italy) of Publius Fannius Synistor, destroyed in the eruption of Vesuvius. Roman, 32 cm x61 cm. British Museum, 1899,0215.3.

How different from classical Athens! There the boast was of produce one had found on the market, and of the haggling over the price.

We have moved forward in time 200 years. Rome, once a country town in central Italy, is now the centre of a world state. Traditionally guided by aristocrats, eventually broken apart by the unbounded ambitions of Julius Caesar (100–44 BC) and others, Rome has crumbled into anarchy. Caesar's adopted son, Octavian (63 BC– AD 14), has under the name of Augustus been accepted as the 'first man' of the republic; his authority has passed to his own stepson and adopted son, Tiberius (42 BC–AD 37), and republic has somehow turned into empire. Romans taxed the whole Mediterranean world, and could afford to buy their luxuries from anywhere in the empire – and beyond. The spices of India and Indonesia crossed the ocean, bound for Rome, and Roman gold went eastwards to pay for them.

Rome had grown fearfully rich – but still retained the power to laugh at herself. Juvenal was only one of the great satirists of that first hundred years of empire. Another, apparently friend and courtier of Nero (AD 37–68) himself, was the novelist Petronius. His *Satyricon* drew a portrait of a whole world, the new rich and the work-shy poor, the slave, the lecturer, the prostitute and the vast landowner. Or so it seems. All too little of the *Satyricon* survives, but the centrepiece of what remains is a lavish dinner, 'Trimalchio's Feast', a mockery of the wealth and pretension of imperial Italy. The narrator, Encolpius, is an educated vagabond who has managed to get himself an invitation:

> Now some really high-class appetizers came in. We had all got on our couches by this time – only our host was still missing. Trimalchio was going to take the place of honour himself. Latest fashion? Anyway, on the trolley there was a Corinthian bronze donkey with panniers on its back, green olives in one, black in the other. Over the top of the donkey were two trays. Along the edge of them it said: 'Property of Trimalchio' and '*x* pounds silver'. These two dishes were joined together by little bridges soldered on, and they contained dormice glazed in honey and rolled in poppy seeds. There were sizzling sausages, too, on a silver grill – and, under the grill, damsons and pomegranate seeds.

As in a second-rate restaurant, the effort went into display: the food was showy and expensive (Roman cuisine, thanks to this episode, will be forever associated with dormice glazed in honey and rolled in poppy seeds), but not especially good. Encolpius and his disreputable friends crept away at midnight, leaving their host Trimalchio still drinking.

For better or worse 'Trimalchio's Feast' is the fullest description of a Roman dinner-party that we

55 | Silver-gilt pepper-pot in the form of a sleepy African slave. He is guarding a chained chest (of spices?) between his knees. Roman Gaul: from the Chaource treasure, a wealthy family's silver service, deposited *c*. AD 270 near a French village that is now better known for its cheese. H. 9 cm. British Museum, 1889,1019.16.

can now read. Luckily there is plenty of other evidence from which we can build up a picture of the usual routine.

As in Greece, many houses had a special dining room, the *triclinium*. Three couches, each large enough for three diners, were arranged in a U-shape surrounding a central table. A house with a big enough garden might well have a garden dining area, too, shaded by vines and creepers, with three stone couches sloping gently upwards to the middle – to be made comfortable with cushions and pillows. The open side of the square was for waiters to come and go.

Roman women and children had never dined separately from the menfolk as in Greek families. In the old days, it was said, they sat demurely at the foot of their husband's or father's couch; by the time of the empire they had become used to reclining. Servants took off guests' sandals as they reclined, and brought water to wash their hands. A sequence of dishes began with the *gustatio*, appetisers or *hors d'oeuvres*, followed by a sweet aperitif (see the first recipe in this chapter). These appetisers might be more varied and more costly than the main course, though not so bulky. We know of a religious dinner, attended by Julius Caesar, at which sixteen *hors d'oeuvres* awaited the priestly celebrants. They ranged from sea-urchin and clams to venison and wild boar. The main courses were accompanied by bread and wine. Servants must have been forever coming and going, bringing new courses, clearing away, supplying more perfumed water for finger-rinsing: for diners ate with their hands, with the occasional help of a knife. Music and dance, performed by slaves, might well accompany the drinking, which tended to continue

56 | Woman drinking on a balcony. The image probably suggests the libation of wine that is poured when a traveller sets out. Vignette from a Roman wall decoration, Rome, early 1st century AD. 60 cm x 45.2 cm. J. Paul Getty Museum, Los Angeles, 96.AG.172.

57 | A reclining woman, perhaps a Naiad. She drinks from a gold *rhyton*, a vessel in the shape of a drinking-horn. Roman wall painting, *c.* AD 30–50, from Stabiae (Italy), the smallest of the three towns buried in the eruption of Vesuvius. 29 cm x 46 cm. British Museum, 1867,0508.1356.

long after the meal itself was over. A napkin, which lay in front of the diners as they reclined, might serve as a knapsack to take home the little gifts of food or wine with which a host would regale his friends as they departed.

We have not quoted a long list of main courses – read Petronius' *Satyricon* for plenty of examples – but the impression may remain that a Roman dinner was an expensive affair. It seems right to end, therefore, with a letter in which Pliny the Younger (born *c.*62; nephew of the encyclopaedist) teases a friend with a menu of the dinner-party that he missed.

> Dear Septicius Clarus: You promise, but you don't turn up to dinner, I'm afraid! All ready and waiting were a lettuce (each), three snails, two eggs, porridge, with *mulsum* and snow (yes, I must count in the snow, right away, because it melted on the plate), olives, beetroot, gourds, bulbs and a thousand other

58 | Wine set from the eastern Mediterranean, late 1st century BC, around the time of the Roman conquest. The two cups are modelled with cupids holding garlands; the handle of the pitcher ends in a satyr's head; there is a wine cooler, a ladle, and a beaker modelled with cupids playing musical instruments. The ring is also Greek in style, but the gold diadem in the foreground is Roman. Silver, dark green chalcedony, gold and glass. H. (of pitcher) 21.5 cm. J. Paul Getty Museum, Los Angeles, 75.AM.54–61.

things no less enviable. You could have listened to comic actors or a poetry reader or a lyrist, or, such is my generosity, all three. But you chose to go to someone else's, and what did you get? Oysters, sows' wombs, sea-urchins, and dancing-girls from Cadiz!

By the early empire – 150 years after the famous Opimian vintage – the wines of Italy were a serious study. Names like Caecuban and Falernian were famous in poetry. But wine snobbery led rich gourmets like Lucullus (117–66 BC) to prize the expensive, boiled-down, sweet export wines of Greece above their own. The custom grew of serving several kinds of wine in sequence at a single party. Pliny writes:

Greek wine was so prized that one would serve just one cup each at a dinner. 'As a boy,' Varro tells us, 'Lucullus never attended a banquet at his father's house at which more than a single cup of Greek wine was served. Well, on his own return from service in Asia Minor, Lucullus distributed more than a hundred thousand jars of Greek wine as gifts!' Caesar, at his triumphal dinner as dictator, provided an amphora of Falernian and a small jar of Chian to each table; but at the feast in his third consulship it was Falernian, Chian, Lesbian, Mamertine. That was the first time, apparently, that four kinds of wine were served.

'I'm giving you real Opimian,' Trimalchio boasted improbably at his dinner table. 'I didn't serve such good stuff yesterday, and my guests then were much better class.'

59 | The great silver dish from the Mildenhall treasure (Roman Britain, 4th century AD). The main frieze is a dancing procession of satyrs, maenads and other followers of the wine god Bacchus. In the centre is the head of Neptune, with dolphins in his hair. The inner circle consists of sea-nymphs riding mythical marine creatures. Diam. 60.5 cm. British Museum, 1946,1007.1.

SPICED WINE

Making *Conditum Paradoxum*. 15 [lb] honey are put in a bronze jar which already contains 2 pints wine, so that you boil down the wine as you cook the honey. This to be heated over a slow fire of dry wood, stirring with a stick as it cooks: if it begins to boil over it is stopped with a splash of wine; in any case it will simmer down when the heat is taken away, and, when cooled, re-ignited. This must be repeated a second and a third time; then the mixture is finally removed from the brazier and, on the following day, skimmed. Next 4 oz ready-ground pepper, 3 scruples mastic, 1 dram each bay leaf and saffron, 5 roasted date stones, and the dates themselves softened in wine to a smooth purée. When all this is ready, pour on 18 pints smooth wine. If the finished product is bitter, coal will correct it.

Apicius I, I

The Romans traditionally served a honeyed wine as an aperitif with the first course at dinner. It was known as *mulsum* and was simply a mixture of honey and wine in a ratio dependent on personal taste. The honey was boiled so that it could be skimmed, but I find that this is less necessary with modern honey. For *mulsum* add 4 oz (½ cup/120 g) clear honey to a bottle of medium-dry white wine: warm the honey slightly so that it will dissolve in the wine. Chill before serving. The *Apicius* recipe, however, is for something finer: a special spiced wine or *conditum*, distant ancestor of modern aperitifs such as Martini. The recipe seems much too sweet, but the intended quantity of honey

60 | Roman amber-coloured glass carafe for wine or water. Roman Britain, 1st century AD. British Museum, 1923,0605.1, donated by W. Gordon Ross.

is not clear in the manuscripts. A Greek recipe for *conditum* suggests a much smaller proportion: 'Making *conditum*: washed, dried, finely ground peppercorns, 8 scruples. Attic honey, I pint. Old white wine, 4 or 5 pints.' This is my excuse for reducing the quantity of honey considerably in the following recipe, though in other ways it is based on *Apicius*.

Mastic is a resin that has been exported from the Greek island of Chios for at least two thousand years. It has a very strong and distinctive flavour, familiar to many Greeks because traditionally they have chewed it to clean the teeth and freshen the breath. *Mastikha*, a spirit similar to ouzo but flavoured with mastic, is widely marketed in Greece. If you want to include mastic it can be bought from traditional herbalists such as Baldwin's in the UK (see page 30 for the address) or from Greek delicatessens.

Makes 6 glasses

---

1 bottle (70 cl) medium-dry white wine

6 oz (³/₄ cup/170 g) clear honey

¹/₂ tsp ground black pepper

1 bay leaf

Pinch saffron powder or strands of saffron

Pinch mastic (optional)

1 fresh date, the stone roasted for 10 minutes and the flesh soaked in a little wine

Put 5 fl oz (²/₃ cup/150 ml) of the wine in a saucepan with the honey and bring it to the boil. Skim if necessary. Repeat and remove from the heat. Add the seasonings to the wine while it is hot: this speeds up the flavouring process. When it is cold, add the rest of the wine and allow to stand overnight. To serve, strain through a fine sieve or muslin.

CHICKEN SALAD (SALA CATTABIA)

Another, Apician *sala cattabia*: put in a mortar celery seed, dried pennyroyal, dried mint, ginger, coriander leaf, seeded raisins, honey, vinegar, oil and wine. Crush. Put in a pan bits of Picentine bread, layered with chicken meat, kid's sweetbreads, Vestine cheese, pine kernels, cucumbers, dried onions chopped fine. Pour the liquid over. At the last moment scatter snow on top and serve.

Apicius 4, 1, 2

There is an interesting combination of flavours and textures in this ancient salad, which is ideal as a first course. I think of it as one of the most successful dishes in *Apicius*. Lamb's sweetbreads are particularly suitable for the contrast of texture. The ancient method is a little vague: I settled on a completely lined mould, as for an apple charlotte or summer pudding, and turn it out before serving. Vestine cheese was a smoked goat's milk cheese marketed by the Vestini, a mountain people of Abruzzo in central Italy, and it was one of Rome's delicacies. My choice of Pecorino Romano, a sheep's cheese very like Parmesan, is a personal one: it is dry with a pungent flavour that contrasts well with the other, milder, ingredients of the salad. You could use a mature Cheddar, or even fresh Parmesan.

Picentine bread, from the same region of Italy, was made in a special way. The recipe involves leaving soaked semolina to ferment for nine days before baking; the earthenware pots in which the dough was placed broke in the oven during baking. The bread, which was white and very light in texture, was always eaten soaked in milk or wine. Substitute a white, sliced, grain-enriched loaf. You will need a 2-pint (5-cup/1.2-litre) pudding basin or similar bowl to make the salad.

8 slices grain-enriched white bread

2 chicken breasts, cooked and diced

4 oz (120 g) lamb's sweetbreads, cooked and diced

3 oz (85 g) Pecorino Romano cheese, grated

1 medium onion, finely diced

4 tbsp (60 g) pine kernels

1/2 cucumber, peeled and finely sliced

Dressing

1 in/2.5 cm fresh root ginger, finely sliced

1 large handful of fresh coriander

2 tbsp (60 g) raisins

1 tsp chopped fresh or 1/2 tsp dried mint

1 tsp chopped fresh or dried pennyroyal (if not available, increase the mint)

1 level tsp celery seeds

3 tbsp (45 ml) red wine vinegar

5 fl oz (2/3 cup/150 ml) red wine

1 tbsp (30 g) honey

3 tbsp (45 ml) olive oil

Salt and pepper

Sprigs of parsley

To prepare the dressing you will need a pestle and mortar. Pound the ginger, coriander and raisins to a pulp – this will take some time. Add the remaining herbs and celery seeds and mix well. Flush the mortar out with the vinegar and transfer to another bowl. Add the wine, honey, oil and seasoning.

Remove the crust from the bread and cut each slice into 3 oblong pieces. Line a 2-pint (5-cup/1.5-litre) pudding basin with the bread as for summer pudding and cut a circle of bread to put in the bottom. Prepare the salad ingredients. Place a quarter of the chicken meat in the bottom of the dish. Follow this with an equal amount of the sweetbreads, cheese, onion and pine kernels. Pour a spoonful of the dressing over the ingredients and add a layer of cucumber. Repeat until you have used up all the ingredients.

Finish with a layer of cucumber. Cover with a saucer, place a weight on top and chill thoroughly. When ready to serve, release the bread from the edge of the dish with a palette knife and turn it out on to a plate. Decorate with cucumber slices and sprigs of parsley.

STUFFED GOURD

Stuffed gourd *hors d'oeuvre*. Carefully cut oblong shapes from the sides of the gourds, hollow them out, put in cold water. Make the following stuffing for them: crush pepper, lovage, oregano, moisten with fish sauce, crush cooked brains, beat raw egg and add to make a smooth mixture: blend with fish sauce. Fill the aforesaid gourds, not fully cooked, with this stuffing, close them with the cut-out pieces, boil, drain when cooked, slice, fry. Make an *oenogarum* thus: crush pepper, lovage, moisten with wine and fish sauce, blend with raisin wine, put a little oil into the saucepan and let it boil. When it has boiled, bind with starch, pour the *oenogarum* over the fried gourds, season with pepper and serve.

Apicius 4, 5, 3

Gourd is not easily available to us: marrow, squash and pumpkin, quite unknown to the Romans as they come from Central and South America, will serve as substitutes. Marrow and squash are seasonal vegetables, available from July to October, and should be chosen with care. Look for young ones, no more than 12 in (30 cm) long, with tender skin. As a first course this recipe is also successful with courgettes (zucchini). The stuffing is made with lamb's brains but minced (ground) lamb, or even beef, will do as well.

Serves 6 as a starter; 3 or 4 as a main course

I small marrow or large yellow squash or 4 courgettes (zucchini)

Olive oil for frying

Stuffing

8 oz (225 g) lamb's brain, sweetbreads or minced (ground) lamb

1 egg

1/2 tsp ground lovage seed

2 heaped tsp chopped fresh or 1 1/2 tsp dried oregano

2 tbsp (30 ml) fish sauce

1/2 tsp ground black pepper

Cut an oblong in the marrow, squash or courgettes, just as described in the ancient recipe above, and hollow out the flesh (keep the oblong cut-out). Push a spoon beyond the edges of the hole to make a large cavity, but do not break the skin. If you are using a marrow or squash and have a large enough saucepan, plunge the vegetable in boiling water for 10 minutes and refresh in cold water. If a large enough pan is not available, put the marrow or squash in a deep-sided ovenproof dish, pour in boiling water till it is half-covered, then cover with foil, bake in a

Sauce

5 fl oz (²/₃ cup/150 ml) red wine

2 tbsp (30 ml) fish sauce

5 fl oz (²/₃ cup/150 ml) raisin wine

2 tbsp (30 ml) olive oil

1 tsp chopped fresh lovage or celery leaf

¹/₂ tsp ground lovage seed

Plenty of ground black pepper

A little cornflour (cornstarch) to thicken

pre-heated oven at 350°F (190°C/gas mark 4) for 20 minutes and refresh in cold water. There is no need to cook courgettes at this stage.

The lamb's brains or sweetbreads should be soaked in cold water to remove any blood, trimmed of any fibres or bone. Place them in boiling water and bring back to the boil for 5 minutes, drain and refresh in cold water. Remove the outer membranes and chop roughly. Combine all the ingredients for the stuffing in a food processor and mix well. Stuff the marrow or squash, pressing the mixture into the hollowed-out ends. Replace the oblong cut-out and tie it securely with kitchen string. Return the vegetable to the saucepan, cover with water and simmer for 1 hour; alternatively place in a deep ovenproof dish with enough water to come half-way up the sides of the vegetable, cover with foil and bake in the oven at 400°F (200°C/gas mark 6) for a similar time. Courgettes will take no more than 30 minutes.

When cooked, drain and allow to stand while you combine the ingredients for the sauce. Bring them to the boil, simmer and reduce a little while you fry the stuffed vegetable. Remove the string and carefully cut into ³/₄-in (2-cm) slices. Heat olive oil in a frying-pan, place the slices in the hot oil and seal each side for 2 to 3 minutes. For a starter arrange slices on a plate and spoon a little of the sauce over the meat.

SHOULDER OF PORK WITH SWEET WINE CAKES

Shoulder of pork with must cakes. Boil the cured pork with two pounds of barley and 25 dried figs. When it has boiled, take off the meat, singe its fat on a red-hot griddle and dip in honey. Better, put it in a bread-oven and coat it with honey. When it has browned, put in a saucepan raisin wine, pepper, a bunch of rue, wine; blend. When blended, pour half of this sauce over the pork and the other half over bite-sized pieces of must cakes. When they have steeped, pour over the pork any that was not soaked up by the cakes.

Apicius 7, 9, 3

Must cakes to be made thus: two gallons of bread-wheat flour to be moistened with must; add to this anise, cumin, 2 lb lard, 1 lb cheese, and grate in the bark of a bay twig; when you have shaped them, put bay leaves under them while you cook them.

Cato, On Agriculture 121

This is an excellent dish for a special dinner: I have often prepared it for Roman banquets. The sweet wine cakes needed some thought. Fresh must begins to ferment almost as soon as it is pressed but does not prove an effective leaven. I believe that, though no proving time is given, Cato's cook expects these cakes to rise. The grape juice that can be bought today in supermarkets is inactive and of no use here. I have experimented with wine with better results, but a really light and absorbent texture is not obtainable today without a little yeast.

Serves 6

Sweet Wine Cakes

8 oz (2 cups/225 g) plain (all-purpose) flour

2 oz (2 tbsp/60 g) pastry lard (such as Cookeen)

2 oz (60 g) Pecorino Toscano cheese, grated

1 tsp ground cumin

Sweet Wine Cakes

To make the sweet wine cakes, sift the flour and rub in the lard. Add the cheese, cumin and aniseed. Bring the wine, with 1 bay leaf, to body temperature and dissolve the yeast in it. Remove the bay leaf. Add the warm wine to the flour. Form a soft dough and knead well. Divide into 6 portions and mould each into

1 tsp aniseed

3–4 tbsp (45–60 ml) red wine

Bay leaves

Pinch of fresh yeast or ¹/₂ tsp instant dried yeast

Gammon

1¹/₂ lb (675 g) piece of gammon or smoked ham

8 oz (2¹/₂ cups/225 g) pearl barley

10 dried figs

1 celery stalk

2 bay leaves

10 peppercorns

8 oz (1 cup/225 g) honey

Sauce

10 fl oz (1¹/₄ cups/280 ml) red wine

10 fl oz (1¹/₄ cups/280 ml) raisin wine

2 tsp dried rue in a muslin bag or a good sprig of fresh rue

¹/₂ tsp ground black pepper

a bun shape. Place on a greased baking tray with a bay leaf beneath each one. Cover with a cloth and leave to rest and rise in a warm place for 1½ hours. Bake in a pre-heated oven at 375°F (190°C/gas mark 5) for 25 to 30 minutes until risen and golden.

Gammon

Leave the meat soaking in cold water overnight. Discard the water and place the meat in a large saucepan, cover with fresh cold water and add the barley, figs, celery, bay leaves, peppercorns and 4 oz (¹/₂ cup/ 120 g) of the honey. Bring to the boil, skim and simmer for 1 hour. Pre-heat the oven to 400°F (200°C/gas mark 6). Remove the meat from the saucepan and retain the liquor. Cool the meat slightly before coating the fat with the rest of the honey. Place in the oven for 30 minutes.

Sauce

Meanwhile prepare the sauce. Place the wine, raisin wine and 5 fl oz (²/₃ cup/150 ml) of the cooking liquor in a pan with the rue and pepper. Bring to the boil and simmer to reduce slightly. To serve, strain the barley and figs from the reserved cooking liquor and arrange them around the meat on a large serving plate. Break the sweet wine cakes in half and, on another plate, pour half the sauce over them. Pour the rest of the sauce over the meat, then arrange the cakes on the serving plate along with any sauce that they have not absorbed. Carve the meat at the table.

61 | Heracles, wearing a lionskin and armed with a sling, kills the Stymphalian birds (here depicted as swans) – the sixth of his Twelve Labours. Athenian amphora, black-figure pottery, Attica, Greece, mid-6th century BC. H. 40.6 cm. British Museum, 1843,1103.40.

PARTHIAN CHICKEN

Parthian chicken. Open the chicken at the rear and spreadeagle. Crush pepper, lovage, a little caraway, moisten with fish sauce, blend with wine. Arrange the chicken in a Cuman dish and put the sauce over it. Dissolve strong asafoetida in warm water; pour over the chicken as you cook. Serve seasoned with pepper.

Apicius 6, 9, 2

This is a simple dish, and very unusual in a Roman context, for it contains no sweetener. It is interesting that it is named after Parthia, Rome's rival in the Middle East, and notable that asafoetida is the dominant flavour. This may confirm that the recipe was Parthian in origin – or at least it may explain how it got its name – for asafoetida came to Rome from the Parthian Empire. Caraway, on the other hand, is of central European origin. It was certainly the Romans who added this to the dish.

Serves 4

4 pieces chicken (breast or leg)

Ground black pepper

6 fl oz (³/₄ cup/170 ml) red wine

2 tbsp (30 ml) fish sauce

¹/₂ tsp asafoetida powder or 5 drops asafoetida tincture

2 tsp chopped fresh lovage or celery leaf

¹/₂ tsp ground lovage seed

2 tsp caraway seeds

Place the chicken in a casserole dish and sprinkle it liberally with pepper. Combine the wine, fish sauce and asafoetida, add the lovage and caraway seeds and pour over the chicken. Cover and bake in a pre-heated oven at 375°F (190°C/gas mark 5) for 1 hour. Halfway through the cooking time remove the lid to brown the chicken. Serve with a little of the sauce poured over the meat.

STUFFED KIDNEYS

Grilled kidneys are made as follows: They are cut down the middle to spread them out, and seasoned with ground pine kernels and very finely chopped coriander and ground fennel seed. Then the kidneys are closed up, sewn together, wrapped in caul, parboiled in oil and fish sauce, and then baked in a crock or on a grill.

Apicius 7, 8

This is another one of my favourite dishes, excellent as a first or main course. At a food tasting of mine one of the 'guinea-pigs', a conservative eater, actually thanked me for curing him of a lifelong hatred of kidneys.

Serves 4

---

8 lamb's kidneys

10 fennel seeds, roasted for 5 minutes in a moderate oven

4 oz (²/₃ cup/100g) pine kernels

1 generous handful of fresh coriander

1 level tsp ground black pepper

2 tbsp (30 ml) olive oil

2 tbsp (30 ml) fish sauce

1 pig's caul (optional)

Skin the kidneys, split in half and remove any fibres. In a mortar, pound the fennel seeds to a coarse powder. Add the pine kernels to the mortar with the coriander. Continue to pound the mixture until it is of a uniform texture. Add the pepper. Place a spoonful of the mixture in the centre of each kidney and close them up. If you can obtain pig's caul from a butcher, use it to wrap each kidney to prevent the stuffing from coming out. Otherwise sew up with a little cotton thread or secure with a cocktail stick. Combine the oil and fish sauce in a frying-pan and heat. Seal the kidneys for 2 minutes on each side, then transfer them and the sauce to a small baking dish and finish in a pre-heated oven at 350°F (180°C/ gas mark 4) for a further 15 minutes. Serve as a first course or as a light snack.

62 | Hellenistic memorial relief, marble, Smyrna, Asia Minor (now Turkey), 2nd century BC. The dead
man is depicted at a family meal, his wife seated at the foot of his couch. There is food and wine
on the table; two children or slaves are in the foreground. 52.1 cm x 45.7 cm. British Museum,
1805,0703.468.

63 | Cecrops, mythical king of Athens, accepts a cup of wine from which he will pour a libation. Athenian wine-cup (of the same shape as the cup that is depicted in this vignette), terracotta, c.480 BC. H. 13.3 cm; diam. (with handles) 40.7 cm. J. Paul Getty Museum, Los Angeles, 84.AE.569.

HONEYED MUSHROOMS

Place the chopped stalks in a new baking-dish, adding pepper, lovage and a little honey. Blend with fish sauce and, sparingly, oil.

Apicius 7, 13, 6

Mushrooms were a prized delicacy in ancient times – but there were dangers involved in eating them. Not everybody knew how to distinguish the poisonous kinds from those that were good to eat. Greek and Roman medical writers therefore suggest many antidotes to mushroom poisoning: illogically, to us, these antidotes often included the ingredients with which mushrooms were cooked. Perhaps the danger was part of the pleasure for the dedicated gourmet, as with the Japanese taste for poisonous sushi. The Roman emperor Claudius (10 BC–AD 54), who began the conquest of Britain (see chapter 7), died in agony after tucking into a dish of *boleti*, but this, everyone said, was not the fault of the mushrooms: his wife had added poison to the dish.

The ancient recipe given above is also for *boleti*. These were not necessarily the kind that is now called boletus (*cèpe*); they were more probably *Agaricus caesarius*, close to our common champignon mushrooms. In any case they were evidently regarded as a delicacy, since the trouble was taken to serve the stalks separately. I find that large open mushrooms are best for this recipe, though you can certainly use dried *cèpes*. These mushrooms are easily prepared as an accompaniment to many of the main course dishes in the book.

Serves 4

---

1 tbsp (15 ml) olive oil
1 tbsp (15 ml) fish sauce
1 tbsp (30 g) honey
1/2 tsp ground lovage seed
1/2 tsp ground black pepper
8 oz (22 g) large open mushrooms, thickly sliced

Combine the oil, fish sauce and honey in a pan and bring to the boil. Add the lovage and pepper and the sliced mushrooms. Cook out briskly in order to reduce the liquids so that, when you serve, the fish sauce and natural water will have been boiled away and the honey and oil give a glaze to the mushrooms.

7 ON HADRIAN'S WALL

Rome's world empire stretched from the banks of the Euphrates to the western shores of Lusitania (Portugal), from the Libyan desert to the marshy banks of the lower Rhine. The Roman army, which had conquered most of this huge territory, was now the empire's guarantee against unrest and invasion. An army of something like half a million men was a miracle of organization. The infrastructure that supported it had a great influence on life throughout the Roman provinces, an influence that in many ways can still be traced today.

Paved Roman roads arrowed from capital to provincial town and onwards to the frontier fortresses. Many routes were studded with official staging posts: at first no more than inns where messengers could change horses, these often grew into centres of local trade. Standard army rations, and standard officers' luxuries, travelled hundreds of miles, by cart and river barge, to reach distant units. Taxes were dispatched inwards, army pay and retirement bonuses were sent outwards, swelling a monetary economy: at last a standard maximum price, empire-wide, could be fixed for all the necessities of army life.

There were few inns in classical Greece, if Greek texts are anything to go by. By contrast, inns are part of the story of Roman life. The inns

of Italy come to life in a narrative sketch by the poet Horace (658 BC): 'We made straight for Benevento, where an attentive host almost burnt his inn down while spit-roasting some lean thrushes for us! A stray spark from dying embers in his old kitchen flew up and set the ceiling alight. Hungry guests and nervous slaves were in competition, rescuing the dinner and putting out the fire.' Then there is a scrap of conversation, found by archaeologists where it was written as an advertisement on an inn wall to catch the traveller's eye:

'Innkeeper, how much do I owe you?'
'There was the wine, twopence halfpenny; bread, a penny; relish, twopence.'
'That's right'.
'The girl, eightpence'.
'Right'.
'Hay for your mule, twopence!'
'That mule will be the ruin of me.'

The first attempt to incorporate distant Britain among Rome's provinces was made by Julius Caesar. His two raids, in 55 and 54 BC, achieved nothing. The fourth emperor, Claudius, however, succeeded where Caesar had failed. The emperor himself spent only a fortnight in the cold wet province, but the invasion he ordered in AD 43 had resulted, within sixty years, in the conquest of all of south Britain as far as the Solway Firth and the River Tyne. Indeed, Roman troops penetrated at times far into Scotland.

Three or sometimes four Roman legions were stationed in Britain. Far from the traditional wine-producing districts of Europe, Romans in Britain demanded wine to drink, lentils to eat, walnuts, figs and olives to chew. All these were imported, and experiments were certainly made with planting vines and walnuts. Roman soldiers and civilians expected familiar flavours in their food, the celery and carrot, the fennel and coriander, the pears, peaches and mulberries of the warm south. Their demands have made a lasting difference to the food and drink of Britain, for all these and many other fruits, vegetables and herbs were introduced to the island in Roman times and in most cases have grown here ever since.

We know this from archaeology, not from literature. The Romans wrote very little that survives about their most northerly province. But writings of Romans in Britain have come quite unexpectedly to light. At one of the forts on the northern border – Vindolanda, in the remote valley of the south

Tyne, close to where Hadrian's Wall would soon be built – a collection of letters, official and private, written in ink on thin sheets of alder wood and discarded around AD 100, has been excavated and painstakingly deciphered. One is an invitation to a lady's birthday party. Another seems to be a day-book recording food supplies issued to soldiers: 'June 24. Barley, 12 gallons; beer, 6 gallons; wine, 3½ gallons; vinegar, 2 pints; *muria*, 1½ pints; pork fat, 15 pints.' The influence, then, was not all one way: somebody at Vindolanda required twice as much beer, the strange malted brew of Gaul and Britain, as traditional wine!

Roman provinces had their own specialities in food and wine, some of them well known across the empire. The island of Crete, for example, was in Roman times the place for medicinal herbs. Fish sauce came from the Mediterranean coasts of Spain and Gaul.

The wines of Greece and Italy were both famous, but the wines of Gaul, the Rhineland and Spain were beginning to develop a reputation. Pliny surveys the wines of Narbonensis (Provence and Languedoc), describing what are evidently ancestors to the aperitifs of today: 'Between Pyrenees and Alps is Marseilles, with wine of two styles: one of them, called "sappy", is made particularly rich for mixing with others. The reputation of Beziers is confined to Gaul. On the other wines of Narbonensis I will say nothing: they have set up a factory to produce them, altering the flavour with smoke, and (I wish it were not so) with herbs and noxious drugs. One merchant even falsifies the flavour and colour with aloes.'

With a menu based on this chapter, good traditional-style French or Spanish wines will go very well. The fortified wines of the Mediterranean shores – Malaga, Maury, Rivesaltes – probably preserve something of the ancient style (though Romans did not literally fortify their wines). There are long-established dessert white wines from here too, Valencia, Muscat de Frontignan and others.

65 | Two silver spoons, one in the shape of a duck, dedicated to the Roman forest-god Faunus. Roman Britain, from a treasure found on Gallows Hill, Thetford, Norfolk in 1979. L. (of longest spoon) 9.2 cm. British Museum.

CUCUMBER DRESSING

Cucumber: pepper, pennyroyal, honey or raisin wine, fish sauce and vinegar. Sometimes also asafoetida.

Apicius 3, 6, 3

Serves 6

¹/₂ cucumber, peeled and thinly sliced

1 tsp chopped fresh or dried pennyroyal (or mint)

2 tbsp (30 ml) raisin wine

1 tbsp (15 ml) fish sauce

1 tbsp (15 ml) red wine vinegar

2 drops asafoetida tincture or 1 pinch asafoetida powder

Arrange the cucumber in a dish; combine the other ingredients and pour over. Cover the dish with plastic wrap and refrigerate for a couple of hours to marinate.

66 | Roman free-blown glass jug of a natural blue-green colour. Britain, 2nd century AD. H. 22 cm. British Museum, 1883,1213.295.

VITELLIAN PEAS

Vitellian peas (or broad (fava) beans). Boil and stir the peas till smooth. Crush lovage, ginger, and to the seasonings add hard-boiled yolks of egg, 3 oz honey, fish sauce, wine and vinegar. Put all this in a saucepan with the crushed seasonings. Add oil and leave to boil. Add to the peas, and stir again if still firm. Add honey and serve.

Apicius 5, 3, 5

Serves 4

8 oz (225 g) marrowfat or other dried peas or

1 lb (450 g) fresh broad (fava) beans

³/₄ in (2 cm) fresh root ginger

¹/₂ tsp ground lovage seed

¹/₂ tsp ground black pepper

3 cooked egg yolks

3 tbsp (90 g) clear honey

2 tbsp (30 ml) fish sauce

5 fl oz (²/₃ cup/150 ml) white wine

3 fl oz (¹/₃ cup/80 ml) white wine vinegar

1 tbsp (15 ml) olive oil

Soak the peas overnight in cold water. The next day strain, place in a pan and cover with fresh cold water. Bring to the boil and simmer for 1–1½ hours until tender, adding extra boiling water if necessary. When cooked, drain and beat until smooth. Alternatively, allow to cool, then blend in a food processor. Leave to one side. If using broad beans, cook them in boiling salted water for 4-6 minutes or until tender, then drain and puree.

You will need a pestle and mortar to make the sauce. Peel and chop the ginger and pound with the lovage and pepper. Add the cooked egg yolks and continue pounding until you have a smooth paste. Add the honey and fish sauce and stir till smooth. Flush out the mortar with the wine and vinegar and transfer to a saucepan. Add the oil, bring to the boil and simmer gently for a few minutes. Add the contents of the saucepan to the peas (or beans) and reheat. I find the peas now sweet enough, so I omit the final addition of honey given in the original recipe.

WHITE SAUSAGES

Sausages: husk grains of emmer, boil together with the liquid in which intestines have cooked and with finely-chopped white of leek. When boiled, remove from the heat. Mince fat and bits of meat and mix all together. Crush pepper, lovage, 3 eggs; mix all this, in the mortar, with pine kernels and whole peppercorns. Moisten with fish sauce. Stuff intestines. Boil and grill briefly or just boil: serve.

Apicius 2, 5, 3

White sausages were traditionally served with a grain or pulse (legume) pottage. I find the recipe for Vitellian Peas (page 143) excellent as an accompaniment.

Serves 6

1 leek (white part only), finely chopped

2 tbsp (30 g) cracked wheat

12 oz (340 g) minced (ground) belly pork

¹/₂ tsp ground lovage seed

2 eggs

2 tbsp (30 g) pine kernels

2 tbsp (30 ml) fish sauce

1 tsp black peppercorns

¹/₂ tsp ground black pepper

Sausage skins

Put 5 fl oz (²/₃ cup/150 ml) water in a pan with the finely chopped white of leek. Bring to the boil and simmer briefly. Sprinkle the cracked wheat into the water and cook out for 5 minutes. Strain and turn out into a bowl and allow to cool. Combine all the ingredients in a food processor and mix well. Stuff the sausages (for advice see Smoked Sausages on pages 108–9) and twist the individual lengths into a spiral. Place the sausages in a pan of cold water, bring it slowly to the boil and simmer for 20 minutes. They will at this stage be white and can be eaten either hot or cold. If you wish, you can grill (broil) them briefly to give them colour.

67 | Heracles, having captured the Erymanthian boar (his fourth Labour), delivers it to Athena – whose *aegis* (protective shield) is armed with serpents' heads in this early depiction. Athenian wine-jug attributed to the Lysippides Painter. Black-figure pottery, Attica, Greece, late 6th century BC. H. 22 cm. British Museum, 1836,0244.93.

STUFFED CHICKEN

Stuffed chicken. Draw the chicken from the neck. Crush pepper, lovage, ginger, chopped meat, boiled emmer; crush boiled brain, break eggs in and work into a smooth mixture. Blend with fish sauce and add a little oil, whole peppercorns, plenty of pine kernels. Make up into a stuffing and stuff the chicken (or sucking-pig), so that a little room is left. You can do the same with a capon. Cook, discarding the bones.

Apicius 6, 9, 14

It is not clear in the ancient recipe whether only a capon would be boned before stuffing, or whether that applies to chicken as well. The intricacies of completely boning a chicken may not be to your taste: you can ask your butcher to do it for you (or follow the instructions in a good cookery book such as Mrs Beeton's) or you can treat this simply as a recipe for chicken with stuffing and omit the boning altogether – it will be a great success either way.

68 | Cockerel, the 'waking bird'. Introduced from southern Asia to Mediterranean lands around 700 BC, chickens soon became the typical barnyard fowl and a popular sacrifice. Mosaic panel from Halicarnassus in Roman Asia Minor (now Turkey), 4th century AD. Diam. 43.5 cm. British Museum, 1857,1220.425

1 in (2.5 cm) fresh root ginger

12 oz (340 g) minced (ground) lamb, or 6 oz (170 g) minced (ground) lamb and 6 oz (170 g) cooked lamb's brains

6 oz (170 g) cracked wheat, cooked for 20 minutes and drained

1/2 tsp ground lovage seed

1 level tsp ground black pepper

1 tbsp (15 ml) olive oil

4 tbsp (60 g) pine kernels

2 fl oz (1/4 cup/60 ml) fish sauce

1 tsp black peppercorns

2 eggs

1 fresh chicken, weighing about 2 lb (900 g)

Peel and chop the ginger. Place the cooked brains and/or minced lamb in a food processor along with the cracked wheat, and all the other spices, herbs and liquids. Mix well; add the eggs and process again. If you are using a boned chicken, spread out the skin on a chopping board, arranging the leg and wing pieces in their correct place. Spread the mixture over the breast area and also into the leg and wing cavities. Bring the skin over the stuffing and fold the edges in at each end. Turn the chicken over and rearrange the skin in a chicken shape. Secure the skin flap with a couple of stitches of kitchen string. If you are using a whole chicken, simply stuff the cavity in the normal way. At this stage you can either roast the bird with a little olive oil and salt and pepper; or, if you have a boned bird, you can boil it, as a galantine is normally cooked. Wrap the galantine in muslin to hold its shape and cook for 1½ hours in water to which you have added a bay leaf and a stick of celery.

There is no sauce for this dish, which is very unusual for a recipe from *Apicius*. Follow the recipe for the sauce that accompanies Stuffed Gourd on page 128 if you would like to serve it with a sauce.

PORK WITH APPLE

Minutal Matianum. Put oil, fish sauce and stock into a saucepan: chop leek, coriander, small meatballs. Dice a cooked shoulder of pork (with the crackling left on). Cook all together. Half way through cooking, add cored diced Matian apples. While cooking, pound together pepper, cumin, fresh coriander or coriander seed, mint, asafoetida root; pour on vinegar, honey, fish sauce, a little concentrated must, and some of the cooking liquor: adjust the flavour with a little vinegar. Bring to the boil. When it boils crumble pastry to bind the sauce. Sprinkle pepper and serve.

Apicius 4, 3, 4

Did the Latin name for this dish come from Gaius Matius, friend of the Emperor Augustus, because it was invented in his kitchen or described in his household book? Or did it come from a fine variety of apples, developed by Matius and called 'Matian' after him? These apples grew best around a certain village in northern Italy on the southern foothills of the Alps of Veneto.

Pork and apple have traditionally been served together in Britain for centuries: this is a fitting recipe for us to revive. The herbs and spices were all available in Roman Britain, whether grown here or imported. Even the fish sauce, *garum*, was made in Britain: an archaeological site near London is unmistakably a Roman *garum* factory.

69 | Fruit-picking in the Garden of the Hesperides, the mythical paradise of the far west. Heracles has not yet stolen these golden apples of immortality (his eleventh Labour). Terracotta oil-jar (*lekythos*), Athens, late 5th century BC. H. 19.7 cm. J. Paul Getty Museum, Los Angeles, 91.AE.9.

1 lb (450 g) boned lean pork

3 tbsp (90 g) clear honey

1 bay leaf

5 peppercorns

1 celery stalk

8 oz (225 g) minced (ground) beef

1 small egg, beaten

1 large leek

1 large handful of fresh coriander

1 lb (450 g) small sweet apples

10 fl oz (1¼ cups/280 ml) white wine

5 fl oz (²/₃ cup/150 ml) white wine vinegar

2 tbsp (30 ml) olive oil

5 fl oz (²/₃ cup/150 ml) fish sauce

2 tsp ground cumin

2 tsp ground coriander

1 tsp asafoetida powder or 5 drops asafoetida tincture

2 tsp chopped fresh or 1½ tsp dried mint

Cornflour (cornstarch) to thicken

Freshly ground black pepper

Place the pork in a pan of water with 1 tablespoon (30 g) honey, the bay leaf, peppercorns and celery stalk. Bring to the boil and simmer for 1 hour. Leave to cool in the water. Form the beef into small balls with a little beaten egg to bind them.

Slice the leek, chop the fresh coriander and peel, core and segment the apples. In a large saucepan put the wine, 10 fl oz (1¼ cups/280 ml) cooking liquor from the pork, the vinegar, oil, fish sauce and the remaining 2 tablespoons (60 g) honey. Dice the pork and add this to the pot with the meatballs. Bring to the boil and add the leek, coriander and slices of apple. Simmer for about 30 minutes until the meat is fully cooked. Add the cumin, ground coriander, asafoetida and mint when almost cooked and thicken with a little cornflour. Finish with a generous seasoning of black pepper.

SOFT-BOILED EGGS

For soft-boiled eggs: pepper, lovage, steeped pine kernels. Moisten with honey, vinegar, blend with fish sauce.

Apicius 7, 17, 3

As an aside, here is another example of how ancient cuisine has to be reconstructed from a jigsaw puzzle of evidence. How did classical Greek cooks slice eggs? How were sorbs, the southern European relatives of the rowan berry, made edible? The story of the origin of love, told at Plato's *Symposium* (chapter 2), happens to give the answer to both questions: 'At that,' Aristophanes said, 'the Creator proceeded to cut the spherical beings in half, just like someone cutting sorbs in half ready for pickling, or slicing eggs with hairs.'

Serves 4

---

4 oz (cup/120 g) pine kernels, soaked overnight in a little white wine

½ tsp ground lovage seed

1 tbsp (15 ml) fish sauce

1 tbsp (30 g) honey

1 tbsp (15 ml) white wine vinegar

½ tsp ground black pepper

4 eggs, soft-boiled

Strain the pine kernels and pound or process them to a smooth paste. Add the lovage, fish sauce, honey, vinegar and pepper and continue to pound or process until you have a smooth mixture – at least, I usually serve it very smooth, but it is just as good if the texture remains rather crunchy. Finish the dish as if you were making egg mayonnaise, and garnish with cucumber, dressed as in the recipe on p. 142.

PATINA OF PEARS

Patina of pears. Boil and core pears, crush with pepper, cumin, honey, raisin wine, fish sauce and a little oil. Add eggs to make the *patina*, season with pepper, and serve.

Apicius 4, 2, 35

A *patina*, in Roman cuisine, is a dish that is either set with eggs or includes eggs as an ingredient. It could be sweet or savoury, and the appearance could vary just as much as the flavour. It was originally named after the typical serving dish, a *patina* or *patella*.

This first *patina* (there are more in chapter 8) is a fruit-based egg custard flavoured with cumin. An odd combination, you may think, but it works very well and has been one of my more popular dishes at dinner-parties.

Serves 4

1¹/₂ lb (675 g) firm pears

10 fl oz (1¹/₄ cups/280 ml) raisin wine

2 tbsp (60 g) clear honey

1 tsp ground cumin

1 tbsp (15 ml) olive oil

1 tbsp (15 ml) fish sauce

3 eggs

¹/₂ tsp ground black pepper

Peel and core the pears and chop them roughly. Cook them till soft in the raisin wine and honey. Pass the whole mixture through a sieve or process it till smooth. Add the cumin, oil, fish sauce and eggs and process again till smooth. Pour into a greased casserole dish and bake in a pre-heated oven at 375°F (190°C/gas mark 5) for 20 minutes or until it sets. Serve warm with a sprinkling of freshly ground black pepper.

Trompe-l'oeil mosaic from Roman Italy, 2nd century AD. Fishbones, crab claws, fruit stones, snail shells — the remains of a banquet, permanently depicted on a dining-room floor. Probably a copy of a lost Hellenistic original attributed to Sosos of Pergamum. Vatican Museums.

8 SUPPER AT THE BATHS

The big city, too, had its cookshops, its bars and its taverns. Juvenal made fun of the old men who still frequented the all-night bars at Rome's harbour town, Ostia, as if they were youngsters:

> The Phoenician host, greasy with respectful hair-oil, runs to welcome his guest's approach and calls him 'Master!', why not 'King!' Here's the waitress running to him with her skirt hitched up, already uncorking a bottle. Send to Ostia for him, Caesar, look in the big tavern there: you'll find him lying alongside some brawler, in among sailors and thieves and runaways, with hangmen and coffin-makers and a sodden priest of Cybele, his cymbals strangely silent. In the tavern all are equally free, all drink from a common cup, the couch is barred to no man, the table is no closer to one than it is to another.

We begin to sense the reality of ancient city life as we read a letter by the philosopher Seneca (c.AD 4–65), complaining of what he had to listen to just outside his apartment window: 'pancake-sellers and a sausage-vendor and a confectioner and all the proprietors

of restaurants, selling their wares with miscellaneous shouts, each in his distinctive accent'. What was the daily routine of those who lived in imperial Rome? Romans tended to eat little during the first part of the day: a breakfast, *ientaculum*, was a snack that many did not trouble to take at all, and only the greedy wanted a big lunch, *prandium*. Workers no doubt found a lunch in a tavern or cookshop. Those who survived through patronage (as did many in Rome) attended on some rich or powerful figure, no doubt hoping that there would be something for themselves when he paused for a bite to eat.

The late afternoon and evening were the time for relaxation. There was no better preparation for a big evening meal, the one big meal of the day, than a couple of hours at the baths. It was a favourite occupation that was well provided for. Grand public and smaller private baths clustered all over Rome, fashionable meeting places, ideal locations for informal business discussions. The ritual was itself soothing, the sequence of exercise, steam bath, warm bath, cold bath. Encolpius of the *Satyricon* first caught sight of his future host, Trimalchio, in the exercise room at the baths, where the great man was showing off his wealth: 'Two eunuchs were standing about among the ball-players, one of them holding a silver chamber-pot. Trimalchio snapped his fingers, and the eunuch held out the pot as his master went on playing. After emptying his bladder Trimalchio called for water for his hands, and rinsed his fingers, drying them in a slave-boy's hair.'

The last of our vignettes of the ancient world presents a less ostentatious scene, a conversation at the Baths of Tigellinus (donated to the city of Rome, apparently, by Nero's fearsome minister). As we shall see, attached to the baths were bars and restaurants: a party could easily spend a whole evening there. The extract is taken from an unusual manuscript, a bilingual phrase-book, *Daily Conversation*,

71 | A young slave asleep. Bronze oil-flask, Roman Britain, 2nd century AD. British Museum, 1824,K/Unknown.0.c, bequeathed by Richard Payne Knight.

originally intended for Greeks learning Latin and Romans learning Greek. The imaginary speaker is heading a party of friends. Unlike Trimalchio he has no slaves of his own, but he has come to the baths for an evening of enjoyment and he begins by choosing an attendant: 'Follow us. Yes, you. Look after our things carefully, and find us a place. I'll just speak to the perfumier – hello, Julius, give me incense and myrrh for twenty. No, no, best quality. Now, boy, undo my shoes. Take my clothes. Oil me. All right, let's go in.' After exercise and bathing the friends move on to the restaurant. A party as large as twenty can order a wide variety of starters and main courses (and the author of the phrase book works in as many variations as he can):

'A good bath, sir?'

'This is my party. Mix wine for us and let's recline. For starters give us beetroot or gourd: add some fish sauce to that. Give us radishes, and a knife: and some lettuce and cucumber, with vinegar and fish sauce dressing. Bring us a trotter, a black pudding and a sow's womb. We'll all have white bread. The sauce wants more oil in it. Scale the pilchards before you put them on the table. We'll have pork shoulder and ham and some mustard. Isn't the fish grilled yet?

'Now, then, some slices of venison, wild boar, chicken, hare. Give everybody a portion of cabbage. Slice the boiled meat. Now serve the drinks.

'We've all had a drink. Bring the turtle-doves and the pheasant: bring the udder, and add some *alec*. Let's eat: it's just right. Give us the roast sucking-pig. That's very hot. You'd better carve it. Bring honey in a jug. Bring a fatted goose, and some pickles. Take round some water to rinse people's hands. Bring us yoghurt, if you have any, with honey, and some halva. Cut it into slices and we can share it out.

'That was a good meal. Give the waiters and the servants something to eat and drink, and also the cook, because he has served us well. Come on, let's go out for a walk …'

The recipes that follow, like many of those in earlier chapters, are taken from the Roman cookery book *Apicius*. This unique compilation is believed to date from the very end of the Roman Empire, perhaps about AD 400. Dating such a text is a very difficult matter. Apicius was the name of a legendary gourmet of 400 years earlier, under Augustus: the book we know is clearly named after him, but is any of it actually his? The 'works of Apicius' were a bedside book, it is said, for a rich dilettante in AD 120: did he fall asleep over the *Apicius* that we know? Probably not. Although it demands many expensive ingredients, *Apicius* as we know it is a severely practical book. It is written in lower-class Latin, 'vulgar Latin', not for rich men to read in bed but by cooks (almost certainly slaves) for other cooks to use.

Finally we may wonder what wines were served at the baths of Tigellinus and to accompany the recipes of Apicius. The history of wine in later Rome has still to be written, but it seems that although much wine was imported from Spain, Gaul and Greece, Italians remained proud of their own vintages. All through the empire no

72 | Preparations for a feast. To the left a cauldron contains stew cooking over a wood fire. More wood is being hurriedly fetched in. To the right wine is being poured from an amphora to be mixed in a krater. Marble relief from a sarcophagus, north Aegean, late 2nd–early 3rd century AD. 15.7 cm x 53 cm. British Museum, 1805,0703.457.

author dared to say in so many words that Italian wines were better than Greek. The western Roman Empire fell. The last emperor, Romulus Augustulus, was deposed in AD 476. The Italian statesman Cassiodorus, minister to a Gothic king, was at last bold enough (in a letter to his agent, written about AD 500) to speak the truth: 'The Count of the Patrimony reports that the royal wine cellars are almost bare of *Acinaticum*. Go to the estate-owners of Verona and offer them a price that they will hasten to accept. It is a wine of which Italy may be proud. Clever Greece may boast its various products, its wines mixed with spices or flavoured with sea water, but in all its elaborations it has nothing like this.'

Verona is 'Italy's most active wine centre' according to Burton Anderson's *Wine Atlas of Italy*. Nowadays its wines range from the dry white Soave and dry red Valpolicella to the headier Recioto (a sweet red *passito* made from sun-dried grapes) and Amarone of Valpolicella. The last is a most unusual wine: a red from sun-dried grapes which is powerful, dry, even slightly bitter. Perhaps this venerable wine retains something of the style that so impressed Cassiodorus.

SEAFOOD RISSOLES
WITH A CUMIN SAUCE

Seafood rissoles are made with cigales and lobsters, with cuttlefish, with squid, with langoustes. You flavour the rissole with pepper, fish sauce, cumin, asafoetida root.

Apicius 2, 1

Cumin sauce for oysters and shellfish: lovage, dried mint, fairly generous cumin, honey, vinegar, fish sauce.

Apicius 1, 29 [1, 15, 2]

These rissoles are delicious made with Pacific prawns, scampi, or fresh lobster meat and crawfish tails, all of which are available frozen from any fishmonger. The rissoles are apparently made without any binding ingredient, such as egg. They tend to break up when cooked in the sauce: that is why I add a little egg to hold them together and (as you will probably be using frozen shellfish) a small quantity of breadcrumbs to soak up the excess fluid. The rissoles are ideal as a first course or as a light lunch.

Serves 4

8 oz (225 g) Pacific prawns, scampi, lobster meat (or other seafood)

$^1/_2$ tsp asafoetida powder or 4 drops asafoetida tincture

$^1/_2$ tsp ground black pepper

1 level tsp ground cumin

1 egg

2 tbsp (30 ml) fish sauce

1 tbsp (10 g) breadcrumbs

Flour for dusting

Sauce

5 fl oz ($^2/_3$ cup/150 ml) white wine vinegar

5 fl oz ($^2/_3$ cup/150 ml) white wine

2 tbsp (60 g) clear honey

2 tbsp (30 ml) fish sauce

1 level tsp ground cumin

1 bay leaf

1 tsp chopped fresh or $^1/_2$ tsp dried mint

1 handful of fresh parsley, chopped

$^1/_2$ tsp ground lovage seed

Ground black pepper

Defrost the shellfish thoroughly, drain and pat dry well with kitchen paper. Pound it down in a mortar or process it to a coarse mince. Add the asafoetida, pepper, cumin, egg, fish sauce and breadcrumbs and mix well. Turn out on to a floured board and form into about 12 balls. Roll in extra flour and leave to chill in the refrigerator while you prepare the sauce.

Combine the sauce ingredients in a frying-pan, bring to the boil and simmer briefly. Add the rissoles and poach them gently for about 10 minutes, turning them occasionally. Serve immediately, accompanied by the sauce.

73 | A Roman *patera*, a shallow bronze pan, too delicate and elaborate for kitchen use, probably for serving at a meal. The central roundel, a Medusa head, would be seen only when the *patera* was empty. The handle ends in the head of the god Pan. Roman Britain, 1st century AD. Diam. 24 cm; L. (handle) 14.5 cm. British Museum, 1882,0405.1.

PATINA OF SOLE

Patina zomoteganon. Arrange any chosen fish, uncooked, in a pan. Add oil, fish sauce, wine, a bouquet of leek and coriander. While it cooks crush pepper, rub in a bouquet of lovage and oregano, add the juices from the cooked fish, beat in raw eggs, blend. Empty into the pan, allow to bind. When set, season with pepper and serve.

Apicius 4, 2, 27

This simple dish can be made with any fish of your choice. I find it particularly good with white fish such as sole or plaice.

Serves 2

2 fillets of sole

1 tbsp (15 ml) olive oil

2 tbsp (30 ml) fish sauce

5 fl oz (²/₃ cup/150 ml) white wine

1 bouquet garni of leek and fresh coriander

¹/₂ tsp ground black pepper

¹/₂ tsp ground lovage seed

1 tsp chopped fresh oregano

2 eggs

Place the fillets in a baking dish and pour on the oil, fish sauce and wine. Add the bouquet garni and bake in a pre-heated oven at 375°F (190°C/gas mark 5) for 15 minutes. Remove, drain off the cooking liquor and reserve. In a mortar pound the pepper, lovage, oregano and the cooked bouquet. Flush out the mixture with the cooking liquor and mix in the eggs. Pour this over the fish and return to the oven until it has set. Serve immediately sprinkled with freshly ground black pepper.

74 | South Italian fish-plate featuring two sea perch, two bass and four prawns. Terracotta, Apulia, Italy, late 4th century BC. Diam. 19.6 cm. J. Paul Getty Museum, Los Angeles, 81.AE.132.2.

ROAST DUCK
WITH HAZELNUTS

Alternative sauce for birds: pepper, parsley, lovage, dried mint, safflower, moisten with wine, add roasted hazelnuts or almonds, a little honey, blend with wine and vinegar and fish sauce. Add oil to this mixture in the saucepan, heat, stir with fresh celery and calamint. Make incisions [in the birds] and pour the sauce over them.

Apicius 6, 5, 2

In this dish a mixture half-way between a sauce and a nut crumb coats the meat and creates a wonderfully crunchy texture outside while remaining fluid underneath. The bird can be, as indicated, an open choice. The recipe has a modern Christmassy feel which can be enhanced by the use of a duck, goose or even a pheasant – but I use chicken with equal success.

 Two unusual herbs are called for in the ancient recipe. Safflower is often known as fake saffron: the powder sold today as 'saffron' is more than likely adulterated with safflower. Under its real name safflower is best known to us as a recently developed cooking oil. Calamint, still used in southern Europe as a culinary herb, is hard to find elsewhere; the closely related catmint is rather commoner and it is this that I have used (the Latin name *Nepeta* may, it seems, be applied to either).

6 oz (1¹/₂ cups/170 g) hazelnuts

2 tsp chopped fresh or 1¹/₂ tsp dried mint

¹/₂ tsp ground lovage seed

2 tsp chopped fresh parsley

1 tsp chopped fresh catmint or calamint (if not available, increase the mint)

2 tbsp (60 g) clear honey

10 fl oz (1¹/₄ cups/280 ml) red wine

2 tbsp (30 ml) olive oil

2 tbsp (30 ml) red wine vinegar

5 fl oz (²/₃ cup/150 ml) fish sauce

1 tsp black pepper

Pinch saffron powder or strands

3 lb (1.5 kg) duck, chicken or other bird

Salt

Roast the hazelnuts for 10 minutes in the oven at 350°F (180°C/gas mark 4). Pound or process them to a fine crumb. Add them to a saucepan with all the other ingredients for the sauce and bring slowly to the boil. Place the bird in a roasting pan and season well with salt and pepper. Cut into the breast and leg and open the incisions before pouring the sauce over the bird. Roast in the normal way in a pre-heated oven at 400°F (200°C/gas mark 6) for about 1½ hours. While cooking, repeatedly baste the bird to ensure that the skin is well covered in the nut mixture. As the wine reduces slightly the sauce will form a crust over the breast, which needs to be maintained once it has formed.

75 | Fluted silver bowl from the Mildenhall treasure. A six-pointed star is seen at the centre: at this period the motif had no connection with Judaism. Roman Britain, 4th century AD. Diam. 10.9 cm. British Museum, 1946,1007.17.

PATINA OF ASPARAGUS

Alternative *patina* of asparagus. Put asparagus in a mortar, pound, add wine, sieve. Pound pepper, lovage, fresh coriander, savory, onion, wine, fish sauce, oil. Put purée and spices in a greased shallow pan, and, if you wish, break eggs over it while cooking, so that it sets. Sprinkle ground pepper.

Apicius 4, 2, 6

This is another savoury egg custard, typical of Roman cuisine, that deserves to be rediscovered. Roman gardeners and gourmets were the first to develop the thick-stemmed, delicately-flavoured asparagus with which we are familiar. But early Greeks, and the country people of the Roman Empire, already knew and appreciated *asparagi*, a group of wild plants, closely related to the cultivated variety, whose thinner, greener, young shoots are almost as succulent. Wild asparagus, if you can get it, would give an excellent flavour to this *patina*.

Serves 4

2 bunches asparagus or 4 cans green asparagus tips

1 small onion, finely diced

5 fl oz (²/₃ cup/150 ml) white wine

1 tbsp (15 ml) olive oil

2 tbsp (30 ml) fish sauce

1 handful of chopped fresh coriander

1 tsp chopped fresh or dried savory

¹/₂ tsp ground lovage seed

¹/₂ tsp ground black pepper

4 eggs

Fresh asparagus must first be trimmed and steamed. Cut them down to about 6 in (15 cm) in length and peel the root end. Bind them into a bundle and stand them in a deep saucepan with boiling water half-way up the stalks. Cover with a lid and simmer for about 5–8 minutes until the root ends are tender, then refresh in cold water. Canned asparagus needs simply to be drained.

Now sauté the onion until tender and allow to cool. Place the asparagus and the onion in a food processor and purée; alternatively, pound them down to a smooth mixture. Add the wine, oil, fish sauce, coriander, savoury, lovage and pepper. Pour the mixture into a greased shallow ovenproof dish and break the eggs on top. Bake in a pre-heated oven at 375°F (190°C/gas mark 5) for 10 minutes. Serve sprinkled with freshly ground black pepper.

76 | Hare nibbling at a bunch of grapes. One of a series of roundels in a mosaic pavement from Antioch in Roman Syria, 5th century AD. 257.2 cm x 682.3 cm. J Paul Getty Museum, Los Angeles, 70.AH.96.

PATINA APICIANA

You make *Patina Apiciana* as follows. Pieces of cooked womb, of fish, of chicken meat, warblers or cooked thrush breasts and whatever else is of top quality. Chop all this thoroughly, except the warblers. Mix raw eggs with oil. Crush pepper, lovage, moisten with fish sauce, wine, raisin wine, and set to warm in a saucepan, and bind with starch, after you have added all the chopped meats and let it come to the boil. When it is cooked, remove with its juices, with a spoon, and rearrange in a serving dish in layers, some with peppercorns, some with pine kernels. Place under each layer as a base a sheet of pasta, and on each sheet one ladleful of the meat mixture. Finally pierce one sheet with a reed and place this one on top. Season with pepper. Before you put all these meats with the sauce into the saucepan you should have bound them with the eggs. The kind of bronze dish you need is shown below [the illustration does not survive].

Apicius 4, 2, 14

77 | Francolin, a game bird typical of the eastern Mediterranean. From the border of a mosaic from Halicarnassus in Roman Asia Minor (now Turkey), 4th century AD. Diam. 43.5 cm. British Museum, 1857,1220.426.

This recipe is remarkably similar to lasagne in structure. The pasta sheets or
lagana, a Greek term, are the same type as those used in the Layered Cheesecake
(page 113), which were made from flour (or semolina) and water. I am in no
doubt that this is the precursor of the traditional Italian lasagne. Durum wheat,
now used for pasta, was already widely grown in the ancient world.

Serves 6

10 fl oz (1¼ cups/280 ml)
white wine

10 fl oz (1¼ cups/280 ml)
raisin wine

3 tbsp (45 ml) fish sauce

2 tbsps (30 ml) olive oil, plus
a little extra for brushing

½ tsp ground lovage seed

½ tsp ground black pepper

A little cornflour (cornstarch)

4 oz (120 g) cooked, peeled
prawns

4 oz (120 g) cooked chicken
breast

4 oz (120 g) diced smoked
ham

4 oz (120 g) smoked sausage
(such as those on page 108),
sliced

4 tbsp (60 g) pine kernels

1 tsp black peppercorns

2 eggs

6–8 sheets of plain lasagne
pasta

Combine the wine, raisin wine, fish sauce, oil,
lovage and ground pepper in a saucepan and
bring to the boil. Thicken with a little cornflour
and cook out briefly. Ensure that the prawns
are defrosted and well drained, add them to
the sauce with the meats and reheat. Add the
pine kernels and peppercorns. Beat the eggs
together and stir them into the mixture while
off the heat. Slowly bring back to heat. Have
ready your pasta sheets, cooked if necessary,
and a greased baking dish. Beginning with
a layer of meat, fill the dish with alternate
layers of meat and lasagne in the normal way,
finishing with a sheet of pasta. Brush this
lightly with olive oil and cover with foil before
reheating in a pre-heated oven at 400°F
(200°C/gas mark 6) for 20 minutes.

That wonderful phrase 'whatever else is of
top quality', used in the original recipe, gives
you free rein to choose your own filling. Don't
be tied by my choice, though it was certainly
acceptable to mix fish and meat together.
Plain pasta sheets can be used or you can
make your own by following the recipe for
Layered Cheesecake (page 113) and rolling
them out to the shape of the dish you use.
Allow them to rest for an hour or so before
assembling. We are not told to cook the dish
again before serving, but I always bring it back
to heat in the oven.

MARROW OR SQUASH ALEXANDRIA-STYLE

Gourd Alexandrian fashion. Drain boiled gourd, season with salt, arrange in a dish. Crush pepper, cumin, coriander seed, fresh mint, asafoetida root. Moisten with vinegar. Add *caryota* date, pine kernel; crush. Blend with honey, vinegar, fish sauce, concentrated must and oil, and pour the whole over the gourd. When it has boiled, season with pepper and serve.

Apicius 4, 2, 14

Serves 6

1 small young marrow
or yellow squash

Salt

4 fresh dates, soaked in
a little wine

2 tbsp (30 g) pine kernels,
soaked in a little wine

2 level tsp ground cumin

2 level tsp ground coriander

1/2 tsp ground black pepper

2 tsp chopped fresh or 11/2
tsp dried mint

1/2 tsp asafoetida powder
or 5 drops asafoetida tincture

2 tbsp (60 g) honey

1 tbsp (15 ml) defrutum
(reduced red grape juice)

3 tbsp (45 ml) fish sauce

2 tbsp (30 ml) olive oil

3 tbsp (45 ml) red wine vinegar

Slice the marrow or squash and steam or boil until *al dente* (still firm). Arrange the slices in a baking dish and sprinkle with a little salt. You will need a pestle and mortar for the sauce. Take the stones from the dates and put the flesh in the mortar with the pine kernels. Mash them down to a paste. Transfer to a bowl and add the cumin, coriander, pepper, mint and asafoetida and mix well. Scrape down the mash and add the honey, defrutum, oil, fish sauce and vinegar. Stir into a smooth emulsion and pour over the marrow or squash. Cover with a lid or foil and reheat thoroughly in a pre-heated oven at 350°F (180°C/gas mark 4). Serve sprinkled with freshly ground pepper.

As in the recipe on page 128, we can substitute marrow or squash for the gourds that the Romans grew. This rich sauce complements their mild flavour very well.

78 | Two Bacchic dancers. A shepherd's pack containing fruit or nuts lies disregarded in the foreground; pan-pipes can be seen to the left. One of the two smaller dishes that accompany the great Mildenhall dish (see page 123). Silver, Roman Britain, 4th century AD. Diam. 18.5 cm. British Museum, 1946,1007.2.

NUT OMELETTE

Upside-down *patina* as a sweet. Roast pine kernels and shelled broken nuts; crush with honey, pepper, fish sauce, milk, eggs, a little wine and oil, turn on to a round flat dish.

Apicius 4, 2, 16

No cooking instructions are given in the ancient text, but it is quite clear that this 'upside-down *patina*' is nothing less than a sweet omelette. The fish sauce is there to add the necessary touch of salt, and it can be replaced with salt.

Serves 4

2 oz (1/2 cup/60 g) nibbed almonds

2 oz (1/2 cup/60 g) broken walnuts or hazelnuts

2 tbsp (30 g) pine kernels

1 tbsp (30 g) clear honey

2 tbsp (60 ml) white wine

2 tbsp (60 ml) milk

1 tbsp (15 ml) fish sauce or salt to taste

6 eggs

Ground black pepper

1 tbsp (15 ml) olive oil

Combine all the nuts and roast them in the oven at 350°F (180°C/gas mark 4) for 10 minutes. Pound or grind them down to a uniform texture resembling coarse breadcrumbs. Place in a bowl and add the honey, wine, milk, fish sauce and the eggs and beat smooth. Season with plenty of black pepper. Heat the olive oil in a non-stick frying-pan and pour in the mixture. Cook as for a basic omelette and grill (broil) for 1 or 2 minutes to set the top. Cut into quarters and serve immediately.

79 | Group of children playing with walnuts. Marble relief from a child's burial sarcophagus (his name was Lucius Aemilius Daphnus). Ostia, the seaport of Rome, 3rd century AD. 30.5 cm x 109.2 cm. British Museum, 1865,0103.7.

A NOTE ON GREEK AND LATIN SOURCES

Some of these texts can be found in English translation: we give details of translations, and of the Greek and Latin texts we have used, in the guide to further reading that follows this note.

There were many Greek books about food. Almost the only ones that still survive to be read today are those written by physicians. Then, even more than now, a sensible diet was considered by many to be a guarantee of health. Fortunately the authors of diet books sometimes troubled to give the full list of ingredients for a recommended dish. Attached to recipes above, therefore, the names of Oribasius and Galen occur. Galen was a famous and successful Greek doctor who practised and lectured in Rome about AD 180. Oribasius lived in the fourth century AD; he was personal physician to the last pagan Roman emperor, Julian 'the Apostate' and one of the main characters in Gore Vidal's historical novel *Julian*. Although we have not taken any recipes from it, a much earlier Greek text, known simply as *Regimen*, dating from about 400 BC, is full of fascinating information on the classical Greek diet. It is sometimes said to be the work of Hippocrates, the legendary founder of medical science. It can be read in English. Some of Galen's writings on food, and some of Oribasius' work, can be read in English at last.

The true doyen of food writers is Archestratus, a Sicilian Greek of about 350 BC (see chapter 3). Archestratus' light poem *The Life of Luxury*, a sequence of lively rules on where to look for good fish and how to cook it, was already a rarity in ancient times and is now sadly lost forever; but a later scholar of food history, Athenaeus, an Egyptian Greek of about AD 200, quoted several extracts from the poem which we have been glad to use. There are now two complete English translations of the surviving bits of *The Life of Luxury*.

We have just mentioned Athenaeus' work. His *Deipnosophists*, a treasury of rare texts from earlier times, is also the source we used for recipes from other lost Greek food books. The new English translation by S. Douglas Olson is now almost complete.

Gourmet cookery was probably taken to Rome by Greek cooks. Greeks who wrote cookery books in Rome included Chrysippus of Tyana and Paxamus, said by some to be the inventor of the biscuit (cookie). Their work is known only in scraps, by way of Athenaeus and a medieval Greek farming manual, *Geoponica*, which is now available in translation. Apart from these there are the recipes of Cato (see chapter 5) and other writers on farming.

The cookery of the later Roman Empire, uniting both Greek and Roman traditions, was codified in the one complete surviving cookery manuscript from the ancient world, the well-known *Apicius*. Those who want to see the full range of these recipes can find them quite easily (see page 173). There are several full English translations of *Apicius*, including the recent edition by Sally Grainger and Chris Grocock. In any case, previously published books on Roman cookery have largely been adaptations of *Apicius*. Our aim in this book has been to give a wider view of Greek and Roman food.

PICTURE CREDITS

2   Museo Archeologico Nazionale, Naples, Italy; © The Bridgeman Art Library
24 Illustration by Sue Bird
30 Illustration by Sue Bird
34 National Archaeological Museum, Athens, Greece; © Universal Images Group/Superstock
52 Illustrations by Sue Bird
53 Photo © akg-images
70 Vatican Museums; © De Agostini/Superstock

FURTHER READING

First of all, here are the texts on classical food that can be read in English translation. In this list, LCL means the Loeb Classical Library, which gives the original text parallel with an English translation. This useful series is kept permanently in print at a standard price per volume. It is published by Harvard University Press, Cambridge, Mass.

Apicius See *Apicius*, a critical edition with an introduction and an English translation, tr. C. Grocock, S. Grainger (Totnes, 2006). The best older translation is *Apicius: The Roman Cookery Book* tr. B. Flower and E. Rosenbaum (London, 1961). The translations by J. Vehling (1936, and reprinted) and J. Edwards (1985) are not recommended.

ARCHESTRATUS See *Archestratus: The Life of Luxury* tr. J. Wilkins and S. Hill (Totnes, 1994); S. D. Olson, A. Sens, *Archestratos of Gela* (Oxford, 2000).

ATHENAEUS See *Athenaeus: The Deipnosophists* tr. C. B. Gulick. 7 vols (LCL, 1927–41); now being replaced by *Athenaeus: The Learned Banqueters* tr. S. D. Olson (LCL, 2006–).

CATO See *Cato: On Farming* tr. A. Dalby (Totnes, 1998).

COLUMELLA See *Lucius Junius Moderatus Columella: On Agriculture* tr. H. B. Ash, E. S. Forster, E. H. Heffner. 3 vols (LCL, 1941–55).

GALEN See *Galen on Food and Diet* tr. M. Grant (London, 2000); *Galen: Selected Works* tr. P. N. Singer (Oxford, 1997); *Galen: On the Properties of Foodstuffs* ed. O. Powell (Cambridge, 2002).

Geoponica See *Geoponika: Farm Work* tr. A. Dalby (Totnes, 2011).

HIPPOLOCHUS See vol. 2 of the LCL Athenaeus.

Moretum See *Moretum: The Ploughman's Lunch, a poem ascribed to Virgil* ed. E. J. Kenney (Bristol, 1986). This poem also figures, alongside a good selection of others, in *Roman Food Poems* tr. Alistair Elliot (Totnes, 2003).

ORIBASIUS See *Dieting for an Emperor: books 1 and 4 of Oribasius' Medical Compilations* tr. M. Grant (Leiden, 1997).

PETRONIUS See *The Satyricon* tr. W. Arrowsmith (Ann Arbor, 1959), or tr. J. P. Sullivan (London, 1965), or *Satyrica* tr. R. B. Branham and D. Kinney (London, 1996).

PHILOXENUS See 'The Banquet of Philoxenus' tr. A. Dalby in *Petits Propos Culinaires* no. 26 (1987).

PLINY See *Pliny: Natural History* tr. H. Rackham and W. H. S. Jones, especially vols 4–6 (LCL, 1950–2) and the revised vol. 7 (1980).

Regimen and ***Regimen in Acute Diseases***, both traditionally attributed to Hippocrates. See *Hippocrates* tr. W. H. S. Jones, vols 2 and 4 (LCL, 1923).

Now some modern works. Andrew Dalby's *Food in the Ancient World from A to Z* (London, 2003) is an encyclopedia of classical food and wine. Alan Davidson's *Mediterranean Seafood* (revised edn, London, 1981) is the best source on the fish of Italian and Greek waters, and his *Oxford Companion to Food* (2nd edn, Oxford, 2006) is rich in historical information both ancient and modern.

Sally Grainger's *Cooking Apicius* (Totnes, 2006) is a practical guide to reconstructing Roman dishes from the only major surviving recipe text. As a survey of the daily life of Rome nothing has replaced Jerome Carcopino's *Daily Life in Ancient Rome* (London, 1956, and reprinted). Joan Alcock's *Food in Roman Britain* (Brimscombe Port, 2001) is full of information about this remote northern province. Andrew Dalby's *Empire of Pleasures: Luxury and Indulgence in the Roman World* (London, 2000) maps the foods, wines and aromas of Roman literature. Katherine Dunbabin's *The Roman Banquet* (Cambridge, 2003) focuses on images of feasting in Roman art, while Emily Gowers' *The Loaded Table* (Oxford, 1993) brings out the complications of Roman poets' references to food. Turning to modern Italy, Gillian Riley's *The Oxford Companion to Italian food* (New York, 2007) is much more readable than any encyclopedia has a right to be. Otherwise, modern Italian food and wine are surveyed by Elizabeth David in her classic *Italian Food* (revised edn, London, 1979) and by Burton Anderson in *The Wine Atlas of Italy* (London, 1990); don't overlook David Downie's *Cooking the Roman Way* (New York, 2002).

On ancient Greek food and dining see Andrew Dalby's *Siren Feasts: A History of Food and Gastronomy in Greece* (London, 1996). Note also John Wilkins' *The Boastful Chef: The Discourse of Food in Ancient Greek Comedy* (Oxford, 2000). There is plenty of information about the food and wine of modern Greece in Diane Kochilas's *The Glorious Foods of Greece* (New York, 2001), Rena Salaman's *Greek Food* (2nd edn, London, 1993), Aglaia Kremezi's *The Foods of Greece* (New York, 1993) and Miles Lambert-Gócs's *The Wines of Greece* (London, 1990).

The trade in ancient fish sauce is explored in R. I. Curtis' *Garum and Salsamenta: Production and Commerce in Materia Medica* (Leiden, 1991), but for an up-to-date study of the real nature of fish sauce see Sally Grainger's article 'A new approach to Roman fish sauce' in *Petits Propos Culinaires 83* (2007) pp. 92–111.

QUOTATIONS AND REFERENCES

Introduction The philosophy of music and cookery: *Regimen* (attributed to Hippocrates) I, 18.

Recreating ancient food The comedy cook: Plautus, *Pseudolus* 810–25. The cook who shares his master's taste: Martial, *Epigrams* 13, 220. Fish sauce: Martial, *Epigrams* 13, 102; recipes, *Geoponica* 20, 46. The fate of silphium: Pliny, *Natural History* 19, 39. Raisin wine: Martial, *Epigrams* 13, 106; Pliny, *Natural History* 14, 80–5; Columella, *On Agriculture* 12, 39.

The homecoming of Odysseus Calypso and Odysseus: *Odyssey* 5, 194-201. Alcinous' orchard: *Odyssey* 7, 112–21. 'Never ate a fish': Eubulus 118 (*Epitome of Athenaeus* 25c). Maron's wine: *Odyssey* 9, 204–11; Pliny, *Natural History* 14, 54. Pancakes in Greek poetry: Magnes and Cratinus quoted by Athenaeus 646e, Hipponax quoted by Athenaeus 645c. Circe's *kykeon*: *Odyssey* 10, 233–6. Byzantine scholar on *kykeon*: Archbishop Eustathius of Thessalonica, *Commentary on Homer* 870, 65, compare Plutarch, *Symposium Questions* 7, 1. Carthaginian porridge: Cato, *On Agriculture* 85. *Alphiton*: Dieuches, quoted in Oribasius, *Medical Collections* 4, 6.

The banquet of Philoxenus Philoxenus, *Banquet*: extracts from longer quotations given by Athenaeus at 685d, 146f and 642f. 'Modern scholars': the exception is D. F. Sutton in her *Dithyrambographi Graeci* (Hildesheim, 1989), who, like us, takes Philoxenus of Cythera to be the author. Agathon's symposium: Plato, *Symposium* 176e; 212c–e. Xenophon, *Symposium*. The story of Aristotle's deathbed: Aulus Gellius, *Attic Nights* 13, 5 (with acknowledgements to J. C. Rolfe's translation in the Loeb Classical Library). The later author who liked the wine of Eresus was Galen, *On the Therapeutic Method* 12, 4. Archestratus on *horaion*: Archestratus 38. The curative qualities of cabbage and a recipe for *oxymeli* with salt: Pliny, *Natural History* 20, 81; 23, 60 (from the Greek author Dieuches); Cato, *On Agriculture* 157, 7. The Cornish recipe for barley bread: *Cornish Recipes Ancient and Modern*, compiled by Edith Martin for the Cornwall Federation of Women's Institutes, 5th edn, 1930.

The markets of the Mediterranean Five months' journey: *Periplus of the Mediterranean* attributed to Scylax. The gifts of Dionysus: Hermippus 63 quoted in the *Epitome of Athenaeus* 27e. The law of Thasos: *IG* xii suppl. 347. The Roman scholar who wrote superciliously of Archestratus' appetites is Athenaeus at 116f. On bonito and on wheat bread: Archestratus 13, 4. On Democritus and grape varieties: Pliny, *Natural History* 14, 20. On Tyrian exports: Ezekiel 27, 17–33.

A wedding feast in Macedon Hippolochus, *Letter to Lynceus*: extracts from the longer quotation given by Athenaeus at 128a. Oxyrhynchus cookery book: see *Opsartytika und Verwandtes* ed. F. Bilabel (Heidelberg, 1920). Archestratus on hare: Archestratus 57.

Cato's farm On visiting the farm, selling surplus stock, and preserving lentils: Cato, *On Agriculture* 2,1; 2, 7; 116. Cato's remark on Lucius Veturius: Plutarch, *Cato Major* 9, 6 (with acknowledgements to A. E. Astin's translation in his *Cato the Censor*, Oxford, 1978). On the Opimian vintage and on investment in wine: Pliny, *Natural History* 14, 55; 14, 57. Greek recipe for *plakous*: Antiphanes quoted by Athenaeus 449c
.

The wealth of empire Farm-fresh dinner menu: Juvenal, *Satires* 11, 56-76. Trimalchio's feast: Petronius, *Satyricon* 31; 34. The priestly dinner: Metellus Pius quoted by Macrobius, *Saturnalia* 3, 13, 10–12. The meal that Septicius Clarus missed: Pliny the Younger, *Letters* 1, 15, 1–4. Fashions in wine: Pliny, *Natural History* 14, 95–7. Greek recipe for *conditum*: *Geoponica* 8, 31 (attributed, implausibly, to Democritus). Vestine cheese and Picentine bread: Pliny, *Natural History* II, 241; 18, 106.

On Hadrian's wall Horace at Benevento: Horace, *Satires* 1, 5. The gaming table: *CIL* 9, 2689 ('penny' in the translation stands for the Roman copper coin *as*). The day-book: no. 190 in Alan Bowman and J. D. Thomas, *The Vindolanda Writing-Tablets* (London, 1994), but they are wrong to translate *acetum* 'sour wine for soldiers'; because of the small quantity, the meaning is certainly 'vinegar'. Foods introduced to Britain: see J. Grieg, 'Plant foods in the past' in *Journal of Plant Foods* vol. 5 (1983), pp. 179–214. The flavoured wines of Provence: Pliny, *Natural History* 14, 68. Slicing eggs: Plato, *Symposium* 190d.

Supper at the baths The all-night bars: Juvenal, *Satires* 8, 158–80. Street sounds and smells: Seneca, *Letters* 56, 2. Trimalchio at the baths: Petronius, *Satyricon* 27. The baths of Tigellinus: compare Philostratus, *Life of Apollonius of Tyana* 4, 42. The conversation: *Kathemerine Homilia* formerly attributed to Pollux (ed. A. Boucherie [Paris, 1872]: 'yoghurt' and 'halva' are approximate equivalents only for *colostrum* and *gelonianum*). The wines of Verona: Cassiodorus, *Variae* 12.4.

INDEX